T0209333

HOW WE MANAGED A TRIO OF BUSINESS VENTURES

HOW WE MANAGED A TRIO OF BUSINESS VENTURES

The story of one family's success in three different businesses in spite of some challenges

Barbara C. Alleyne

HOW WE MANAGED A TRIO OF BUSINESS VENTURES
THE STORY OF ONE FAMILY'S SUCCESS IN THREE DIFFERENT BUSINESSES IN SPITE OF SOME CHALLENGES

iUniverse books may be ordered through booksellers or by contacting:

iUniverse
1663 Liberty Drive
Bloomington, IN 47403
www.iuniverse.com
844-349-9409

ISBN: 978-1-6632-2677-8 (sc)
ISBN: 978-1-6632-2678-5 (e)

Print information available on the last page.

iUniverse rev. date: 09/17/2021

CONTENTS

About The Author vii
Dedication...xi
Foreword.. xiii

Chapter 1   Seeking A New Path.....................1
Chapter 2   Targeting A Market – Location ...4
Chapter 3   Researching The Project..............8
Chapter 4   Developing The Plan 11
Chapter 5   Financing 15
Chapter 6   Securing A Place To Do
             Business 17
Chapter 7   Flick City Video – The First
             Venture.......................................20
Chapter 8   Confectionary Corner – The
             Expansion....................................36
Chapter 9   Sale of Flick City Video 48
Chapter 10   Tropical Isles Gourmet
             Deli – The Second Venture.........56
Chapter 11   The Grand Opening....................62
Chapter 12   Closure of Tropical Isles by
             Eminent Domain 69

Chapter 13 Real Estate –
          The Third Venture......................79
Chapter 14 Tenant No. 1 84
Chapter 15 Tenant No. 2 87
Chapter 16 Tenant No. 3 91
Chapter 17 The Eviction...............................102
Chapter 18 A Recession Sets In 107
Chapter 19 Tenant No.4 115
Chapter 20 The Recession Continues –
          Our Plans Change 123
Chapter 21 Tenant No. 5 125
Chapter 22 Tenant No. 6 136
Chapter 23 The Other Properties................142

Summary 147

ABOUT THE AUTHOR

Barbara Alleyne was born and raised in the Island of Barbados, British West Indies. One of seven children, she had an early exposure to entrepreneurship when her father who was a Police Sergeant in the Barbados Police Force would plant and cultivate a variety of vegetables on his days off from work. She and her older siblings had to assist their mother with the task of pumping water from the family's well to water rows of carrots, beets, cabbages, cherry tomatoes, string beans, and lettuce on their mini farm. Eventually, her father bought a windmill and rotating pipes to lighten the task of having to pump water from the well every day. Some of the vegetables were sold to market vendors that came to the family's home. Besides the vegetables, her mother had a small variety shop next to the family's main home. Barbara would help in the shop when she was on vacation from school.

Barbara attended private elementary and secondary schools. After graduating from high school, her father wanted her to pursue a career in nursing just like her eldest sister who worked as a nurse at the Barbados General Hospital prior to migrating to the United States in 1955 to advance her nursing career. Barbara was not interested in becoming a nurse. Instead, she got a job as a statistics clerk with the Barbados City government, working in the mayor's office. After two years with the City Government, she was invited to join her sister in the United States. Once again, her father suggested that she should consider nursing as a career. Her sister tried to persuade her. However, Barbara preferred to pursue a career as a secretary. While in the States her sister got her enrolled in a business school in New York City. She studied shorthand and typing for several months and eventually received a business certificate.

After receiving her permanent residency, she got a job as a secretary at the YMCA Headquarters in New York City working for the executive in charge of development and fundraising. Her secretarial responsibilities included taking minutes for the weekly board meetings. She also had the responsibility of compiling annual membership reports for several branches of the organization. Although her position entailed a significant amount of philanthropic work which Barbara enjoyed, the organization did not offer tuition refund for college.

Barbara wanted to advance her education to get a college degree. To this end, she applied for a position with the Ford Foundation in New York City since the Foundation offered 100 percent reimbursement for college. Additionally, the Foundation also offered a significantly higher pay and a wider range of benefits including free medical, four weeks' vacation profit sharing, etc. She accepted a position at the Foundation as an administrative assistant in the office of Program Related Investments. She said that working at the Ford Foundation was one of the most pleasant job experiences she had. Barbara completed both her AA and BA degrees while going to college at night and some weekends.

During the mid-1970s just before the end of the Vietnam War the country was in a recession. The Foundation was one of the companies that was affected by that event. The consequence was retrenchment. To counteract the possibility of job insecurity, she sought and accepted a more secure position as an administrative secretary at the Texaco Oil Company headquarters which at the time was in the Chrysler Building in Manhattan. The company was in the process of relocating to a new facility in Harrison, a suburban town in Westchester County, New York.

After working as an administrative secretary for several years she was promoted to a position as a Contributions Assistant in the company's Public

Relations Department. In this position Barbara reviewed and did write ups on applications that were submitted to the company for grants. These write ups were then discussed at weekly meetings to determine which applicants should receive a grant. Barbara also worked with the company's scholarship program which offered over 300 scholarships to eligible employee's children.

Over a period of several years, Barbara volunteered to work with various community outreach programs that the company supported. These included United Way Campaign and Blood Drives. She also served as President of the Texaco Forum, a women's group that also supported some of these programs.

Her husband also worked for Texaco as a Graphic Designer. She has one son who works for the U.S. government as an air safety investigator.

DEDICATION

*This book is dedicated
to the loving memory of my
parents and siblings*

FOREWORD

When I made the decision to give up working for a fortune 500 company, I was not sure if I had done the right thing. Leaving the corporate arena meant that I would be giving up a wealth of experience coupled with some great benefits. Nevertheless, the time had come when I felt I had enough of some of the unfair practices that existed within the company. With the support of my husband who recognized how stressed I was becoming due to the prevalence of these inequities I was able to gather the determination to break away from the situation that was causing me anguish.

Once I started my own business with my family, the difference between working for a corporation where I had to adhere to protocol that I may at times disagree with and making decisions where I know that they were the right ones for me became quite clear.

CHAPTER 1

Seeking A New Path

After working for a large fortune 500 corporation for several years, I became weary of some lower managers who, for an unjustifiable length of time, tried to hinder my ascent to a higher rung of the promotion ladder even though I had two degrees and more than seventeen years of experience with the company. The reason was obvious- I was a minority female working in a male dominated atmosphere.

I loved my job, and they were several co-workers with whom I had a good working relationship. I also participated in a variety of community outreach programs that were sponsored by the company. As a result of the reorganizing of some departments in the company my job was assigned to this specific group. It was difficult for me to accept the change. Consequently, I became frustrated and increasingly experienced a flurry of thoughts about how I should deal with the situation.

On several occasions I discussed my discontent with the changes that had taken place with my husband. In our discussions, I expressed my desire to pursue a different path in the business world. Although he worked for the same company as I and had a similar experience of unfair practices, he had a greater level of tolerance than I did. He encouraged me to stay the course because he felt that a change for the better would eventually come. Besides as he reminded me, the company had many outstanding benefits. As time went on, I could not envision that a change would come. Subsequently, I became consumed with conflicting ideas about what I should do in my desire for job satisfaction.

My son, who was in the air force at the time, suggested that perhaps I should consider starting a family business. Although starting a family business sounded like a good idea at the time, I could not imagine what kind of business I could pursue. In a family discussion, it was agreed that if I did consider starting a family business it would have to be something that I would not only enjoy, but one that would also be lucrative to really make it a worthwhile venture. He said that he would sometimes rent movies to watch on his days off. From his observation of how busy the store was when the customers were there, it seemed that it might be a fun business to pursue.

The movie rental business was booming during the time he was completing his military assignment (1986) and he offered to explore the ins and outs of the business for me. The information he garnered confirmed that the movie rental business was becoming a new form of entertainment and family members of all ages could watch movies from the comfort of their living or family rooms. The time was the 1980s. Going to the movies was becoming expensive at that time since there was also the popcorn, ice cream and candy to buy. Renting a movie for one night was much cheaper than taking a family to see a two-hour movie at the theater.

CHAPTER 2

·※※※·

Targeting A Market – Location

The Target Market

The idea of transitioning from the world of corporate business to becoming an entrepreneur at first seemed somewhat far-fetched. However, after getting as much information as I could about the video rental business. I became more excited at the video store idea and felt that it may be a worthwhile effort to pursue this path. In a discussion with my husband, we both concluded that before deciding to pursue this path we should first determine the following matters:

- How much would it cost to start a video rental business
- What target market should we pursue

- What location would be best for the business
- What legal requirements would have to be fulfilled to set up business in a specific location

Accomplishing the goal of targeting a specific market would be critical because prospective consumers would be significant for achieving success in the business. We understood that to identify a specific target market for this venture would require a definitive study of the group(s) most likely to rent movies on a regular basis.

Armed with this information we then had to determine the areas that were replete with the target market we would want to reach. This was not a difficult task because all age groups everywhere were renting movies. Gathering this significant information then paved the way for us to forge ahead with our plans to fully pursue the goal of business ownership.

Location

While it is critical that a prospective business owner target the specific market that he or she would want to reach for the establishment and eventual success of a business, equally important is the location in which that prospective owner sets up the business.

We scoured several areas we believed would be an ideal location for our prospective business venture. Although it was not easy to find the perfect spot, eventually we found a location with an open parking lot that could hold about thirty automobiles. Additionally, there was some street parking that would be available for customers. In addressing the subject of location, it was also necessary to think about what distance we would be from competitors.

When we surveyed the location that would be ideal for a movie rental store, we discovered that there were about three movie rental stores, within a two to three- mile distance from the area that we were considering. Seeing that the competition would not be far from the location where we would be we then had to think about how we could possibly compete with already established video store owners in both volume of product and service being rendered to consumers. Since the specific location that we were considering was replete with several young families who were the ones renting movies on a regular basis we felt that would give us an advantage so long as we could maintain a standard for quality of service and customer satisfaction.

Bearing in mind that we would be threading in unchartered waters we decided to proceed with plans to open a video store. We felt confident that we would be pursuing a worthwhile business and that we should do well once we could focus on and accomplish the goal of customer satisfaction. But to further move closer toward our goal, we first had to do some general research into what steps we would need to take for the start-up of a business.

CHAPTER 3

·※※※·

Researching The Project

While doing research about the requirements for starting a business it became quite clear that an integral component of this research should include an effective study of market trends which should entail information about the steps that are necessary to start a business. One interesting fact that we found out during our research was that some new businesses fail during the first year of operation. Since our prospective business would fall into the new category when it is opened, we wanted to know the root cause(s) for the failure of new businesses since we would not want to encounter the same predicament.

We had a meeting with a gentleman from an organization called SCORE. This organization was run by a group of retired business executives whose goal was to give advice to new and prospective business owners. At the meeting, we learned that insufficient capital and inadequate business acumen were among the reasons why some businesses fail, especially after a short period of time (sometimes during the first six months to one year after opening). There are other businesses that are successful well after years of operation.

In the research we learned that it was necessary to first develop a business plan which, among other things, would help us determine if the business we were pursuing would be suitable for our personalities. Even when a plan is executed, there could be variables along the way which would require an adjustment to make the effort worthwhile.

We acknowledged that while it is not an easy task to run a successful business, with the right mind set coupled with patience and determination to work hard toward a set goal it can be done. Initially we had no idea about the right business for us to pursue. At times we felt somewhat hesitant to cherish the idea of business ownership especially when, during the research, we heard stories about new businesses that failed during the first six months to one year of operation. At times we also felt that it may be too risky to venture into the realm of business.

To temper our fear of the unknown we made a concerted effort to get information from owners whose stores were several miles from the location we were considering. Most of them were, understandably, reluctant to share any information with us. A few gave us vague ideas about how their businesses were faring in a highly competitive video rental market. We went into some stores to make observations on how some owners were handling their rentals and customers, the number of customers that came into the stores and the busy times and days, as well as daytime renting as opposed to evening renting. We frequented some stores at various times and on different days to accomplish this feat. These observations gave us a good idea about the operations of the video rental business. One store owner let us spend more than an hour in his store to observe the rental traffic during the busy times and how he handled it.

CHAPTER 4

※※※

Developing The Plan

When we reviewed the notes on information that would help us determine how we should proceed in this venture, at times we were still not quite sure if the video rental business is the right type of business we should consider. Our son reminded us that since the video rental business was rapidly becoming the new form of entertainment for the whole family, we should give serious thought to pursuing it. Some additional information he gathered for us was instrumental in helping us make the decision to consider this type of business. Before we made the final decision however, we first had to find out what we needed to do for the start-up of a video rental store and what was the best way to proceed in this effort.

Utilizing some of the ideas we gleaned from the marketing and management courses we took while in college, it became clearer to us that to effectively pursue the goal of starting our own video store it was necessary to develop a business plan that would outline the process to follow for the start-up of the business. Our plan included:

- Determining the appeal for movie rentals
- Targeting the right age group(s)
- Selecting a viable location for the business

Legal Requirements

Other major aspects of our plan were centered on the following:

- Finding out if it would be legal to operate a business in the location we were targeting
- Should we be established as a corporation or partnership
- What license we would need for the store

Permits

In laying out our plan we learned that a special permit was needed to operate a video rental store in the city where we would be doing business.

Sales Tax

In addition to a permit to do business, we would also have to obtain a tax collection certificate to collect sales tax on any item that we sell or services we may render.

Tax I.D. Number

An employer tax ID number would be required for the purpose of declaring business income as well as payroll taxes if we decided to hire employees.

Banking

For information on banking, we contacted our bank about the type of account we would need for depositing daily business income. Also, since the use of a credit card was a requirement for renting movies, we needed to know the monthly fees that would be required for us to utilize the bank's system to check the validity of a customer's credit card.

Accounting

We were referred to an accountant who gave us advice about the most proficient method to use for keeping track of the daily cash intake when the business is set up. He suggested that we could maintain a general ledger for that purpose. We could also utilize his services for preparing our annual business tax returns.

CHAPTER 5

※※※

Financing

Business can have seasonal ebbs and flows therefore we had to be certain that we would have adequate finances not only for the start-up but also to sustain the business especially during the first critical year. Before making a final decision to proceed with our plan, it was critical that we establish the following:

- Financial output needed to start-up-the business
- Would we have adequate capital in case of a seasonal drop in business activity
- At what stage should we expect to see significant growth in the business
- Rent
- Equipment
- Supplies
- Utilities (Gas, Electricity, water)
- Insurance

- Medical
- Telephone

Realizing that unforeseen circumstances can occur at any time, especially in a new venture, we wanted to ascertain that we had the financial resources to sustain any unforeseen lapse in business. After approximating and evaluating what our financial output would be to start with, we consulted with our financial institution to determine our chances of getting a business loan. Even though we would be providing a sizeable portion of the funds for the business, it was decided that we were not eligible for a business loan. Our alternative then was to take out a home equity line of credit. We, instead decided to finance the startup with other investments we had accrued.

Prior to making the final decision to proceed with our first business venture and to be sure we were on the right track, we consulted with our attorney on the various aspects of our plan. In the discussion about the pros and cons of the business it was determined that it would be more advantageous to us that the business be established as a corporation rather than a partnership. We agreed to let our lawyer handle all the paperwork required to obtain the permits we would need to operate in the city where we would be doing business.

CHAPTER 6

Securing A Place To Do Business

Once our business plan was fully laid out and we got all the information about the requirements needed to start up a video store, we contacted a leasing agent about an empty store in an area with several stores except a video rental store. There was not much activity in the area when we met with the agent. Nevertheless, we believed we would do well in the location since most of the businesses were frequented by young families which was the market we wanted to reach.

After a discussion about the type of business we would be operating, he explained in detail the requirements for renting the store - deposit, monthly rental, length of lease, etc. After meeting with him two more times to discuss how the store would have to be configured should we decide to lease it, he scrutinized our credentials.

Subsequently, he agreed that we did meet the qualifications for leasing the store.

While the store was in an area that was ideal for the business, the front of the building was in dire need of repair, especially the display window which was somewhat smashed in. When we asked the agent about its condition, he said that the landlord was in the process of renovating the front of the store. He assured us that the renovation would be completed by the time we were ready to occupy the space. Furthermore, he continued, the owner had a planned renovation which would include some of the other stores that he owned on the same block where our store would be. He said that he would give us a five-year renewable lease. Additionally, since our store would be new, we would get three months rent-free to give us enough time to set up the store for business.

Since this was our first venture, we consulted with our lawyer to discuss the terms of agreement that should be spelt out in the lease. After the final negotiations with the Leasing agent a lease was drawn up for our signature. Before signing, we went over all the details both with the agent and our lawyer to verify that there were no unclear clauses in the document and that the official name of the store Flick City Video was spelled correctly. It was then agreed that the lease was complete and ready for our signatures. After we signed the lease, we were anxious and ready to prepare the store for the start of business.

Since the store space was empty for more than a year, we had to fix the interior to adapt to the requirements for a viable video rental store. For this we retained the services of a builder who got a carpenter an electrician and a painter to construct the necessary shelving for the videotapes, wire and install light fixtures and paint the walls to create the look of a modern-day video store.

Although we spent more than we budgeted for, the finished look inside the store convinced us that the overspending was worth it. Furthermore, we were reminded that the location was the target market area that we aimed for.

While the work inside the store was being done in preparation for the product, we had the arduous task of selecting the list of movies for the grand opening. Three movie buffs assisted us in categorizing the selection which was important to make sure that we had the right variety of movies and categories to start with.

CHAPTER 7

Flick City Video – The First Venture

The name Flick City Video was selected because it reflected an image of the movie industry. After two months had gone by the renovation of the store's facade was not completed as was promised. We acknowledged that there could have been a valid reason for the delay. However, we did not let it deter us from forging ahead with our planned opening date. When we questioned the reason for the delay, there was no definitive answer given.

Our date set for opening the store was January 1,1987 yet up until the end of February we were unable to open because of a further delay. Although we were disappointed about the lack of a logical reason why the space was not ready as was promised, we were determined to open before the end of the rent free three months that were allotted to us. We double checked all the below listed items to ascertain that we would be ready for our grand opening.

DECORATING THE STORE

The store was painted in the following colors:

- Sky blue for the walls
- Royal blue and red shelving to display the movies

Our décor included two large pictures of the New York City skyline, showcasing the Brooklyn bridge and the World trade Center. These posters were professionally framed and were placed on opposite sides of the store.

EQUIPMENT

- A Red and blue neon lighted sign highlighted the front of the store
- A computerized cash register that would be programed for movie rentals and the names of all customers. This system would also help us keep track of every movie that was rented and returned
- A Fax, telephone and answering machine system to help us efficiently communicate

with suppliers that we would be doing business with
- Credit card checking equipment
- Adding Machine - File Cabinet
- Floor racks for some movies
- A special display case to showcase blank tapes for recording tapes, batteries for VCR machines, etc. videotapes and video games for purchase.
- A Video camera with tripod and case.
- TV Monitor for preview of new movies.
- Shelving for the empty movie boxes
- Racks for display of movie boxes in store aisles
- Racks and shelving for storage of movies behind the counter

SUPPLIES

Since this business venture was in the movie rental business, we had to be sure we got all the information needed about how and where to purchase our movies for rental. In our queries about supply sources, several wholesalers were recommended to us. My husband's co-worker who worked in the Information Technology Department had a friend who owned a video rental store.

He was instrumental in advising us where to get our supply of the movies and video paraphernalia that we would need for the business. We had a list of three companies that we would utilize for our supply source. Posters would be included in the purchase of all new movies that were scheduled to be released every week.

The following items were included in our supplies:

- All major new movies that were released
- Video games (Mortal Kombat - Super Mario Brothers)
- Video game equipment (Nintendo and-Genesis)
- Blank VHS Cassette tapes
- VCR Batteries
- Regular batteries (Flashlight, video camera, etc.)
- Boxes for the storage of each movie
- Barcodes
- Printed labels for the movies

OPENING DAY

Once we ascertained that everything was ready for the grand opening, we were all excited. The start-up of our family business in a highly competitive market had finally come to fruition. Our initial stock was five hundred movies. It included all the new movies that were released for the prior month.

On the day of the store opening we, of course, did not know what to expect. We could only hope that everything would go as planned. To our surprise, several people came into the store shortly after the doors were opened. The first weekend of our opening we had an open house. For this we had a table set up with a variety of cookies and other goodies for consumers when they came in the store.

MEMBERSHIPS

Since renting a movie required a customer to join a membership, several people signed up on the first day to become members of Flick City Video. Many of them told us that they were happy to know that there was a video store in their area that was just a short walk or ride from their homes. This was proof to us that we had chosen the right kind of business in the right location. Our membership prices were set at the following rates:

Lifetime.......... $39.95(10 free rentals included)
One Year.........$24.95(6 free rentals included)

Members could reserve new movies up to three days in advance. Additionally, they received a 5% discount on the purchase of any movie that was on sale. Also, they received a free bag of popcorn with the rental of two or more movies at the same time.

MOVIE GENRES

Movie genres were:

- Action Drama
- Suspense Drama
- Action
- Comedy
- Children
- Horror
- Science Fiction
- Foreign
- Classics
- Musicals
- Spanish language
- Adult

The actual movies were placed on special racks behind the showcase They were all numbered and barcoded. In addition to the general movies for rental, we carried instructional videos on the following topics:

- Travel
- How to instructions for repair of simple household items
- Exercise
- Karate

We also carried a limited supply of movies on Laser Disc.

One concern we had at the opening was that while the entrance door of the store had a signal bell to notify us whenever anyone enter the store, we did not yet have the security system installed to protect the inventory at night when the store was closed. Our son made a booby trap board with protruding nails as a break- in deterrent. Every night he would place this board at the inner entrance of the door as a security measure when the store was closed. He would remove this board every morning after opening the store. This procedure went on for one month before we finally got an agency to install a regular security system for us.

A late fee was imposed when the movie was returned late. On a rare occasion, there was a renter that we had to pursue for the return of a movie. To discourage late returns we got permission from our landlord to open a drop slop in the wall of the front of the store to make it convenient for those customers who said that by the time they were ready to return a movie it was either late in the night when the store was closed or early in the morning before the store was opened.

After some movies were rented for a significant number of times they were offered for sale and sometimes they were rented under a free rentals category that we created. Listed below are items that were offered as free rentals:

- The twilight zone TV series
- Martin Luther King civil rights marches that took place in
- Memphis and Alabama during the 1960s civil rights movement
- Music, and Exercise videos
- Meditation and various arts videos

To retain space for new releases, we sold copies of some movies after they were rented several times. To meet the growing demand for new movies we had to extend our budget to buy additional copies of new releases.

The movie rental business was still relatively young during the eighties and early nineties. Memberships grew in leaps and bounds, so did the number of video rental stores that were opening during that time. Stores like blockbuster video was becoming prominent in several communities. As the Movie rental business became increasingly popular and memberships grew significantly, we like several of the large stores, discontinued charging fees for membership.

ADVERTISING

Even though we had a good opening, we continued to have occasional advertising campaigns and offered specials to attract new customers and fortify our presence in a highly competitive business. Sometimes we hired two people specifically to distribute flyers around the neighborhood when major new movies were released. This form of advertising brought many people to the store to sign up for memberships. Occasionally we played short music videos on the large TV monitor we had installed in the store. The coming attractions were also advertised on the TV. Some people enjoyed this promotional tool while browsing. New movies were also showcased on large posters placed in strategic areas of the store. These posters were significant since they had pictures of the major actors on them. Window displays showcased several new movies that were already in the store.

The products and service provided by a business owner should be of the standard that would attract the target market in a big way. Based on the positive comments we got for service to our customers we felt confident that we were on the right track. Satisfied consumers would be repeaters, as well as marketers in a way, since they most likely will tell others about the quality of service that was provided to them. It was therefore imperative that we made going the extra mile to appease a factor in customer relations.

As with everything in life there will be trials and tribulations. Our first trial as a new business was an elderly man who owned a fruit and vegetables store next to ours. He probably was in business for time and eternity. Every day he would park his truck with his supplies right in front of our entrance door in the early evening hours just when the customers were coming in to rent movies for the evening.

Although we could not say for sure, we believed that his actions were racially motivated. Perhaps, he could not tolerate the fact that we, as minorities, had opened a store that was just a stone-throw away from an affluent community in Westchester County, New York. We complained to the landlord about his actions and the landlord got the city to rectify the situation because from what we understood, no truck was ever parked in that spot before Flick City Video was established.

SPECIAL ACTIVITIES FOR KIDS

Movie Essay

Since our membership included several young families with children, we developed a movie contest for children. The first contest was a movie essay for children eight to twelve years old. For this contest they were asked to write a short essay on what they liked most about the Jurassic Park movie with the names of the different dinosaurs they saw in the movie. They were given one week to submit the results of the essay to us. We asked one of our members to read the essays and select the winner. We offered three prizes. The winner got a copy of the movie as the prize. Second and third prizes were a Disney movie. Kids who could not complete the essay were given posters of Disney movies. For the Jurassic Park Movie, we had the display window set up like a park with miniature dinosaurs and small hills. It was a big attraction.

Video Game Contest

Another program that was offered for kids was a video game contest consisting of Mortal Kombat and Super Mario Brothers video games. Children ages ten to thirteen were eligible to participate in this contest. The winner got a free game. The other kids got two free rentals for any game. Our son was the organizer of this contest.

Magic Shows

A magic show was added to the activities for kids. For the show we hired a popular magician to perform a variety of magic acts. The show took place in the children's section of the store and was featured from time to time. There were some adults who also enjoyed the magic acts.

SPECIALTY CARDS

As Flick City Video continued to grow additional products were added to our variety. These items included:

- Basketball Cards (these became a huge collection item for the kids)
- Pods cards
- Marvel comic book cards

VIDEOTAPING OF VARIOUS EVENTS

After we were in business for approximately three years, we expanded our services to include the videotaping of the various events listed below:

A CHRISTENING

Our first videotaped event was the christening of a baby for the daughter of a Brazilian doctor who was a member of our store. He hired us to videotape the full christening of his first grandchild. At the end of the ceremony, he invited us to his home to partake of a Brazilian feast. We had to decline the offer because we had to get back to the store.

NEW YEAR'S EVE BALLS

We videotaped four New Year's Eve balls which were sponsored by a community association in the Town of Greenburgh. Four of these balls were held at the following hotels in White Plains and Tarrytown, N.Y.

Crown Plaza Hotel

Holiday Inn Hotel

Approximately two hundred and seventy-five people attended each of these balls. Tickets for these balls were usually sold out two to three months early as the event became more popular. A sumptuous Caribbean-American buffet was served at these balls. One of the highlights of the evening was a sculpture made of ice with the words and number of the specific New Year. The event culminated with a venetian hour featuring a variety of tantalizing desserts and inspiring drinks.

SUMMERTIME BOAT CRUISES

During the summertime we videotaped several dinner cruises on the Hudson River. These cruises were sponsored by a ministry group from a church in White Plains, New York. Entertainment on the cruise was provided by a popular D.J.

A CONFIRMATION

We received several requests to videotape a variety of functions and events. This time it was the videotaping of the confirmation of a twelve-year old boy. This event was held at a church in the Bronx, N.Y. It was a beautiful sight to see all the kids that were being confirmed.

WEST INDIAN CARNIVAL BALL AND PARADES

One of the most exciting events that we had to videotape was a carnival parade and ball. The three-day event started on a Friday with a children's costumed band parading for best costume prize. Next on the agenda were colorful costumed bands parading for the best costumed band prize at a ball held at the County Center in White Plains, N.Y. The culminating event was a huge Sunday afternoon street parade on Tarrytown Road, N.Y.

Participating in the parade were all the bands from the Friday and Saturday night events, several cars with sponsors, and dancers with costumes depicting various characters. They were all accompanied by a parade grandmaster. The weekend event ended with a finale at the County Center in White Plains, N.Y. featuring all the calypso singers and costumed characters that participated in the weekend activities. It was truly a grand extravaganza to behold.

VCR REPAIRS

A service offered by Flick City Video was the removal of movie tapes that from time to time were returned to the store stuck in someone's VCR. Our son introduced this service to members to avoid the possibility that someone attempting to remove a stuck tape from the VCR could damage both the tape and the VCR in the process. After having to deal with this situation several times he became expert at the procedure.

We usually never charged for this VCR service unless there was obvious mishandling of the movie such as an attempt to make a copy of the movie. If it were discovered that such attempt took place, we would charge a late fee since we would lose some revenue during the time the movie was stuck in the VCR, subsequently out of circulation.

TAPE DEPOTS

We had requests from two corporations asking us to supply them with a select number of movies for the convenience of their employees. These movies were rotated on a bi-weekly basis. The companies welcomed the service that we were providing for their employees.

Flick City Video continued to grow in what appeared to be leaps and bounds. In a quarterly business meeting, we discussed how we had grown in just a few years. While my husband and I were still working and going to the store in the evening some customers expressed amazement when they learned that we had regular nine to five jobs. They asked how we were able to do it.

We were in the store even on Thanksgiving and Christmas days which were some of the busiest days for renting movies because families were all at home and wanted to have a movie or two to watch after dinner.

CHAPTER 8

∗⧚∗⧚∗

Confectionary Corner – The Expansion

By the end of the fourth year that we were in business, Flick City Video had outgrown its space. The opportunity for expansion of the store arose when the occupant of an empty store next to ours had just retired after being in business as a beauty salon for several years. We approached the landlord and expressed our desire to lease the space as soon it was available. The landlord said that he would give us the first consideration for leasing that store since we were already renting the existing store from him.

Once all necessary arrangements were made for leasing the additional space, we were advised that a new lease would be drawn up and incorporated into our existing lease. Additionally, we would be allowed three additional months free rent to fix up the added space. After signing the addendum to our existing lease, we had to gather our thoughts as to how we would execute the expansion. The problem was that now we had two separate stores carrying the same products. We had to determine the best way to take care of the customers that would want to get an item from the additional store space. We were planning to move the children's section to the new area. However, with this new space a customer would have to exit one store to go into the next store. We could not inconvenience customers who were the mainstay of our business.

While getting the additional store was an afterthought, we needed the extra space. Our son had the brilliant idea to make an arc through the wall to create an expansion of the existing store space. This would then make it easier for customers to go from the existing store into the added store space. We decided to approach the landlord and asked if he would allow us to cut an arc in the wall. He said he had no problem with that idea. His main concern was that we would be able to pay the additional rent. Once everyone agreed, we hired someone to cut the arc to make a large space between the two stores.

The additional store was for the expansion of the video section. However, we realized that once the children and foreign movies sections were moved to the additional space there would still be ample space that could be utilized for something else. The new addition was painted in the same colors as the main store. The children's section was adorned with several Disney posters. After giving much thought to how we should utilize the extra space our son came up with the idea of creating a confectionary section. We were not sure how this idea would work but we decided to try it. After researching several confectionary distributors, the final decision was to utilize the extra space for that purpose.

We had a display case custom built for the variety of candy we would be carrying. The company that made the Flick City neon sign for the video store designed a special neon sign with Confectionary Corner emblazoned in red and blue to advertise the new section. Soon after we were ready to receive the first shipment of candy.

The Confectionary Corner was opened in February 1990 with a supply of boxes of Valentine Day chocolates. Since it was Valentine's Day demand for the chocolate was significant. Our candy items included Jelly bellies in a wide array of flavors and colors. They were displayed in attractive hexagon shape glass jars. The assortment of popular candy included:

- Sour Power Straws - Sour Patch kids Lemon Heads
- Jaw Breakers -Airheads – Blow pops – Rainbow pops

- Specialty candy items were:
- Tequila Pops (with a worm)
- Pop rocks that crackled
- Crystal rock candy in different colors and flavors
  Multi flavored fruit slices

Seasonal items included:

- Easter eggs
- Miniature Valentine hearts
- Assorted Halloween candy including candy corn
- Christmas candy canes and Santa chocolates

These items sold amazingly well especially since we were in an area with a middle school and other families with younger children.

Shortly after this section was set up, we purchased a theatrical size popcorn machine like the ones seen at county fairs. With the purchase we received a discount on the price of the popcorn and butter we would need. This became a hot item with the sound and sight of corn popping. Some kids were thrilled when they saw the machine especially since it was near the children's movie section.

Otis Spunkmeyer Cookies

About six months after the confectionary section was opened, a representative from Otis Spunkmeyer Cookie Company came to the store to ask if we would carry their cookies in our store. After giving some thought about the idea we agreed to sell the cookies. The Company provided the cookie machine and the dough for the cookies which were made fresh every day. The cookies we sold were:

- Chocolate Chip
- Peanut butter
- Oatmeal

The most popular of these were the chocolate chip and Oatmeal.

Frozen Yogurt

It was approximately one year after the Confectionary Corner was opened that another company asked us to sell their product. This product was for Dannon Yogurt. In keeping with the trend of the day at that time, it would be another product to add in our Confectionary Corner. Frozen yogurt was popular in the 1990's. We agreed to carry the yogurt in the following flavors:

- Vanilla
- Chocolate
- Strawberry
- All flavors were available in a twist.

The company supplied the yogurt making equipment. The yogurt mixture was delivered to our store once a week and stored in a large commercial refrigerator which was kept in a storage room at the back of the store. As the Confectionary area was expanding, so was the number of customers that would come to buy either cups or cones of frozen yogurt at lunch time, especially during the summer.

Our success with this product drew not only lines of customers but also the ire of one store owner who launched a complaint against us stating that our customers were blocking the sidewalk and preventing regular foot traffic from flowing as it should. One day a town inspector came to the store stating that we should not be selling yogurt because the store was in a residential area that was not zoned for selling frozen yogurt.

Our son was at the store serving customers at the time and he called us at work to let us know what was going on. He said that the inspector told him that we had to remove the yogurt machine and put it somewhere in the back of the store. This inspector also said that he would come back to the store the next day to make sure that we had removed the yogurt machine from the store.

We were terribly upset about this because it did not make sense since a deli a few doors down from us was selling packed frozen yogurt. We felt that this must be a set-up to stop our sales. We immediately contacted our lawyer about the incident. The lawyer called the inspector's office. As it turned out, the inspector was incorrect in telling us to stop selling the yogurt and remove our yogurt equipment from the store.

It was obvious to us that the store owner that complained about the lines of people that were patronizing our store did not want us to succeed in this business. We believed that the issue was racially motivated, but we did not let it deter us from forging ahead with our business. Even when the City's inspection showed that we were in the right, this inspector came back to the store another day stating that he wanted to measure the space where the arc was opened to see if the two spaces were wide enough for a pass-through arc. It was so silly. Another inspector came to the store a few days after. He said that he did not know what the first inspector was talking about. Our lawyer had to call the city to get them to advise this inspector not to come to the store again with obvious evil intent to disrupt our business.

PATTIES

The vibrancy of the Confectionary Corner attracted another vendor. This time it was a solicitation to sell Jamaican meat patties. This product was a variation from what we intended to carry in that area. Although we had the space, we had to get approval from the landlord to sell patties. He said that it would be okay for us to carry the product since they would be frozen when they were delivered to the store. Also, we would not be handling raw meat. We agreed to try the following patties to see how they would go.

- Beef
- Chicken
- Vegetable

As agreed with the vendor the patties were brought to the store frozen once a week. They were placed in our commercial refrigerator and were heated in the same oven that was used to bake the cookies. To our surprise, the patties went exceptionally well. Occasionally, we had a request for cocktail patties which a few customers would request for a party. We would accommodate such a request but only on a limited basis since our focus was not food related at that time.

EMPLOYEE - CUSTOMER RELATIONS

Providing quality service to customers relies not only on the owner's professional attributes, but also on the professionalism of employees. Having the right employees is important because they are the ones that would be handling your customers and selling your product. Employees must know how to handle the customers. A good product in the right location will not matter if an employer does not have the employees to accomplish the goal of customer satisfaction.

Our employees included several young people who were familiar with the trends of the day when it came to movies and video games. Ninety percent of the kids that worked for us were efficient in helping customers select movies because they themselves had seen most of the movies. Our first employee was a high school senior. He was outgoing and had significant knowledge of most of the newly released movies. He was also witty and instrumental in bringing some of the first customers to the store to be signed up as members.

Some of our employees lived within walking distance of the store. Others were driven to the store by parents. We did not allow them to work more than fifteen to twenty hours a week while they were still in school. Many of the fourteen and fifteen years old wanted to work in the confectionary section of the store for obvious reasons – it was lively and vibrant and did not require any special skills to do the job. We showed them how to operate the cash register and how to handle the sales and customers. The young adults ages eighteen and over worked in the video section since they were more experienced and had greater knowledge of many of the movies.

It was now five years since our business was established. My husband and I were still working for the corporation we were with for several years. Working five days a week on my regular job and then going to the store every weekend was becoming a little too much for me. I was also putting together all the orders and doing all the paperwork and payroll for workers as well as interacting with customers while I was in the store.

With the addition of the Confectionary Corner, Flick City Video became the anchor store on the block and most of the consumer traffic at any given time was headed towards Flick City. We were located close to the affluent town of Scarsdale and other nearby cities. Our customers included the former NBA Commissioner and several doctors from the White Plains Hospital just a few blocks from the store.

The year was 1992 and I was close to the age of eligibility for an early retirement package from my public relations job. Since I wanted to spend more time at the store, I had a discussion with my husband and my son about my desire to do so. They both agreed that it was time for me to relinquish the demands of the nine to five routine that was the hallmark of my daytime job. In July 1993 I submitted a request for an early retirement package with full benefits to my supervisor who notified the head of the department of my request. They understood my desire to take early retirement from the company. However, they asked if I could stay until the end of October that year to help with the company's annual report. I told them that I did not want to wait that long because I wanted to focus strictly on the business that my family and I had now built up.

My request was eventually approved and all the paperwork for my package was completed. Shortly after I received my separation papers from the company, it felt a great sense of relief. I now had more time to focus on some things I wanted to do in the store but never had the time to do so. Specifically, I was able to concentrate on getting an upgraded security camera installed in the Confectionary section of the store. This system was an enhancement to the entrance door security chime because it aided a worker who might be working in the store alone during a slow period of the day by allowing that worker to not only see who was entering the store from the door on the Confectionary side but also to verbally communicate with the person as soon as the door was open. My pile of orders, receipts, tax documents, and selection of movie magazines gradually became smaller as I had more time to go through the assortment and clear my files. Best of all I was able to do these things on my own designated schedule.

Two of our suppliers sponsored shows and conferences every year for video store owners. New innovations in the industry were highlighted at these conferences. We attended three of these shows and at one of them we met one of the stars of the movie Ferris Bueller's Day Off. We also got to meet and mingle with some other video store owners. Several of them talked about the success they were having in their stores at the time. One of these shows was held on the USS Intrepid Aircraft Carrier that was docked in the harbor on New York City's West Side.

CHAPTER 9

Sale of Flick City Video

As time went on Flick City Video and its confectionary corner continued to flourish. To many of our customers it was a favorite family store and we interacted with some of them on a first name basis. While in the tenth year of business we were approached by a couple people who said they were interested in buying the business from us if we ever wanted to sell. The thought about selling the business at that time never crossed our minds. The offers came often.

We started to think that perhaps it might not be a bad idea to consider selling since my husband and I were just a few years from full retirement age. Besides, being in the store six evenings every week and most of the day on Sundays and holidays might not have been the ideal thing for us to continue to do. Furthermore, our son, who helped managed the store was about to continue his pursuit of a career in aviation.

This meant that soon he would not be able to give us his full support in some areas of the business.

After receiving three offers from investors, we decided to accept an offer from the highest bidder. With extensive negotiations the business was sold in July 1997.

After the business was sold, we assisted the new owner for two months with the transition by going to the store at his request to get more familiar with the workings of the business and the customers. While we made every effort not to show how much we missed not still being there, it was sometimes hard not to admit that we regretted giving up the business.

Soon after the new owner took over some rumors started to spread that most customers found it hard to adapt to the his modus operandi. We had established ourselves not just as very accommodating to our customers, we also reached out to the community in a friendly and outgoing manner and customers appreciated that.

After we had left the area for some years, we still think of the times we spent at Flick City Video and of the many kids that worked at the store. Several of them we hired when they were just teenagers. They are now grown adults, some perhaps with families of their own. Quite often we also think about those customers who appreciated the service we provided to them.

Throughout the late nineties and the early years of the twenty-first century the movie rental business continued to grow in leaps and bounds. By 2004 technological advancement had propelled the movie rentals business to a pay-per-view system. This new system gave individuals a choice of paying a network to stream movies direct to television screens at home. Shortly thereafter, large cineplex venues in various cities along with a conglomerate of red box systems like those seen at some supermarkets provided even more choices for the movie going public. The system will undoubtedly be catapulted into yet another sphere to benefit future generations of movie goers.

Eric Alleyne preparing the store for the opening of Flick City Video

Victor and Barbara Alleyne at the opening of Flick City Video

Display boxes of new releases and coming attractions

Jurassic Park window display

Jurassic Park Promotion Display

FLICK CITY

Video Club

MEMBERSHIP RATES

LIFETIME **MEMBERSHIP $39.95** (includes 10 free rentals, one per month.)

ONE-YEAR **MEMBERSHIP $24.95** (includes 6 free rentals, one per month.)
(Renewable fee of $15.95 per year)

(Members are entitled to a 5% Discount on purchases)
(Members can reserve movies up to one week in advance.)

MOVIE RENTAL RATES

RENTALS FOR MEMBERS **$2.50** — NON-MEMBERS **$3.99**

$1.95 MOVIE MON. — THURS.

<u>FRIDAY SPECIAL (MEMBERS ONLY)</u>

RENT 3 MOVIES FOR $12.00 AND RETURN ON MONDAY

RENT 4 MOVIES FOR $16.00 AND RETURN ON MONDAY

<u>SATURDAY SPECIALS (MEMBERS ONLY)</u>

RENT 3 or MORE MOVIES AND GET SUNDAY FREE (RETURN ON MONDAY)

.99¢ RENTAL AVAILABLE ON A VARIETY OF MOVIES

DEPOSITS OF $50.00 CASH REQUIRED ON RENTALS FOR NON-MEMBERS

TAPES ARE TO BE RETURNED AT LEAST (ONE) 1 HOUR
PRIOR TO CLOSING THE FOLLOWING DAY
LATE CHARGES—$1.00 PER TAPE PER DAY

Flyer advertising memberships rates

FLICK CITY VIDEO

*VIDEO RENTALS, SALES, ACCESSORIES
& CONFECTIONERY CORNER*

· 1 0 1 9 8 9 ·

Sample of membership card given to customers

Zulu Dawn Floor Display

Floor Display of Maximum Overdrive Movie

*Victor Alleyne working on
advertising material for store*

Customers being served at confectionery corner

CHAPTER 10

·※※※·

Tropical Isles Gourmet Deli – The Second Venture

After our exit from the movie rental business, we were finally able to relax and take more control of our time and daily activities. One thing we always wanted to do but never had the time to plan for because of our busy schedules, was taking an extended vacation so that we could relax for a while and travel to various places that we always wanted to visit but never did because of our busy schedule in the video store.

We were barely settled in our new relaxed mode of living when we were enticed to pursue another business venture. This time it was in the food business. Specifically, a Caribbean style restaurant. Coincidentally, this type of business was one of the ideas we had in mind when we first thought of starting a family business. However, the feasibility of doing so at that time did not

56

appear to be significant. Now with a wealth of experience as entrepreneurs we grasped at the challenge to establish a Caribbean gourmet style restaurant in a major city where there was an abundance of popular food establishments.

After giving some serious thought about whether this was something that we should even consider, we eventually succumb to the idea and decided to take the plunge. As we did in our first business venture, we laid out the research we would do to see if there was a market for this type of food business in White Plains, N.Y. While doing this research we were somewhat surprised to learn that a Caribbean deli would fit perfectly in an area where there was already a variety of food places. The location was perfect since the city was saturated with corporate offices, small retail stores and a variety of food places. With this combination the target market and the location were perfect.

Our next step was to find out what were the city requirements for opening a restaurant In White Plains. This was the same city office where we got our permits to open the video store. Besides all the tax and other permits that we had to get for our first business venture, a food establishment would require additional permits plus a different variety of operational equipment. Without hesitation, we pursued utilizing the services of a realtor to find a place that was available for lease in that area. The agent told us about an empty store, less than a mile from a major shopping mall. that would be the ideal spot.

Eventually we met with the owner of the empty store to talk about the type of business we wanted to put in the empty space. After a lengthy question and answer chat with her about our plans, she readily offered to rent the empty store to us.

Our first thought was that taking on another business venture where we would have to do a total renovation and different configuration of a store might not be wise. But to use the space as a restaurant that is what we would have to do if we really wanted to pursue this venture.

Our financial standing was strong at the time, we knew what had to be done to formulate a plan. Without delay, we told the realtor that we would lease the store if the lease terms were favorable. After meeting once again to discuss what the landlord was looking for as far as monthly rent, length of lease, etc. The landlord said she would allow us six months free rent so we can prepare the place and get all the equipment and permits in order. The decision was then made to have a lease prepared and ready for our perusal and signature. After we read all the lease terms we consulted with our lawyer and went over the lease paying special attention to the clause about fixing up the store the way we wanted it.

Eventually we had the okay to proceed with the signing of the lease.

CONFIGURATION OF THE STORE

To start with the fixing of the space to accommodate a gourmet deli restaurant we were referred to an architect whom we hired to do the drawing and layout for the store. Since the last tenant of this store sold mainly hardware items there was quite a bit of work to be done to transform the space to a food place. However, the architect, a professional who had done work for some companies in New York City, did an amazing job in the layout for the space.

After the architectural layout was completed and approved by the City of White Plains, we entered another phase – the transformation of the store to accommodate the construction of the kitchen, and other areas to be utilized as a restaurant. Our son was referred to a builder whom he contacted about doing the renovations: Listed below are some of the major items that had to be done:

- New walls and flooring throughout the store
- Plumbing for the stove and steam table
- Installation of ceiling exhaust fan over the stove

- Pass through serving window
- Grease Trap
- Installation of AC System
- Bathroom Facilities
- Storage area and shelving for products

Equipment

Listed below is the major equipment that had to be purchased for the kitchen area:

- Six burner Commercial stove with fan
- Prep table for meats – Prep table for vegetables
- Steam Table – Food temperature meter
- Commercial Refrigerator
- Regular sink – Slop Sink
- Cooking utensils – large pots – spoons – knives etc.
- Refrigerator for sodas and other drinks
- Fountain Drink dispenser
- Small oven for heating Patties
- Cash Register
- Chairs, Tables

DECORATING THE STORE

Our color scheme for the interior of the store was a pale yellow. We had a green canopy made with the words Tropical Isles Deli displayed on it. Our display window had the name of the store emblazoned in yellow neon lights.

CITY APPROVAL

Once we had everything prepared for the opening, an inspector came to check that all the equipment installed in the kitchen met the standard for opening a deli restaurant in the city of White Plains. When we received the inspector's approval, we immediately started preparations for the grand opening.

CHAPTER 11

※※※

The Grand Opening

We had flyers made which were distributed to customers at the opening and start of business. As in our first venture, we had an open house for approximately three hours to welcome everyone that came through our door. The set up was a table with a variety of cookies and miniature pastries that were available for all who wanted to partake of them. Coffee was also provided. Once we were fully opened, the store hours were 10 a.m. to 7 p.m. Monday through Saturday. We were closed on Sunday.

In addition to the warm welcome extended to us from everyone who came in the store on the first day, the mayor of White Plains, at that time, also came in and gave us a special welcome. He also invited us to join the Business Group of White Plains. We were eventually invited to a breakfast meeting at the City Council's office where we met other business leaders. They all wished us good luck with the business.

OUR MENU ITEMS

Below is a listing of the menu items that were served at the restaurant:

Meat

Oxtails – Jerk Pork – Curry Goat – Pigtails with Oxtails

Chicken

Jerk (spicy or mild) – Brown Stew – Curry BBQ Wings – Baked – Fried

Fish

Baked Red Snapper – Fried Whiting Curry Shrimp

Side Orders

Rice and Beans – White Rice – Cabbage and

Carrots – Green Salad
Fried Plantains – String Beans

Serving Sizes

All meat and chicken orders were available in large and small sizes. We also had a special lunch box size for those who preferred a smaller dish.

Except for shrimp which came in sizes like the meat and chicken dishes, all other fish orders were one size.

Soups

Chicken – Kidney Bean
Red Snapper - Mutton - Beef

Roti

Chicken – Shrimp – Beef

Patties

Chicken – Beef – Vegetable – Cocktail

Sandwiches

Hard dough Bread and Cheese
Bun and Cheese

Side Dishes and Platters

Macaroni and Cheese – Macaroni Salad
Tuna Salad – Potato Salad
Rice and Beans Platter

Special Orders

Codfish Fritters – Pudding and Souse
Fried Dumplings
Stew dumplings made with Cornmeal

Pastries

Bread Pudding – Coconut Bread – Carrot
Cake
Fruit Cake – Bean Pie – Pecan Pie
Sweet Potato Pie – Pumpkin Pie

Caribbean Drinks and Beverages

Carrot Juice – Irish Moss – Sorrel
Ginger Beer – Ting Sodas – Roots Drink

Sodas and other Soft Drinks

Pepsi – Coke – Ginger Ale – Seven Up - Mountain Dew – Nantucket Nectars – Snapple

Fountain Drinks

Lemonade Fruit Punch

CATERED EVENTS

We had several requests for catering a variety of special events. Listed below are some of the popular ones:

Birthday Parties	Halloween Parties
Mardi Gras Parties	Office Parties
Luncheons	Promotional Functions
Church Clergy Functions	Boat Rides

Black History Month Celebrations

DELIVERIES

We had several daily requests from various office facilities for lunchtime deliveries. To keep up with the demand, we hired a part-time person specifically for this service. Some orders came from corporations that were as far as five miles from the deli.

EMPLOYEES

Our kitchen staff consisted of the following workers:

Head Chef   Food Servers
Assistant Chef Food Preparation

Dishwasher

Since our menu was mainly Caribbean food items, we selected people that were experienced in preparing a variety of Caribbean and American dishes. They also had to have the personality to meet the challenge of customer satisfaction. The benefits for our employees were generous. These included:

- One week paid vacation the first year of employment
- Participation in a medical program if they wanted to
- Uniforms for the Head Chef
- Free lunch for all employees

SUPPLIERS

Our sources of food products were as follows:

Oxtail, pork, chicken was from suppliers in the Hunts Point section of the Bronx:

Fish was mostly from the Fulton Fish Market

Our vegetables were mostly from vendors in the Bronx terminal Market

We utilized two sources for our paper goods (napkins, plates and some spoons and forks. These were in

Portchester, NY
White Plains, NY
Bronx, NY

For our takeout containers, we utilized sources in White Plains, NY

CHAPTER 12

————— ❀❀❀ —————

Closure of Tropical Isles by Eminent Domain

Tropical Isles Gourmet Deli was a thriving business with a perfect location. After four years of operation, our landlord advised us that some developers wanted to acquire the complex of stores by eminent domain to construct a cinema complex, a large hotel and several upscale condos. Unfortunately, Tropical Isles was one of the stores in the complex that they wanted to acquire. We were very worried about the acquisition because if all the other landlords in the adjoining complex of stores decided to sell their stores to these developers, we would have to move to another location or accept a payout for the business.

The idea of having to relinquish the deli was disheartening since we had put so much time and money into the development of this business. Our expenditures included paying an architect a substantial fee to do the drawings for a total renovation of the store. We also had to hire a construction company to install new walls, flooring, and new stairs to the basement where our supplies were stored. For the kitchen, we had to install a new ventilation system. We had purchased tables and chairs for customers who ate in at the deli. Our final décor for the store was an awning with the words Tropical Isles Gourmet Deli emblazoned on it. We also had a lighted neon sign promoting the store.

Negotiations between the developers and the landlords of all the stores in the complex went on for one year before we were finally told that the landlord had to sell all the stores. While we were disappointed, we realized that the landlord could not refuse an offer of millions of dollars for the complex of small stores. When negotiations were complete all the store owners in the other complex were also notified of the date when the demolition would start.

Just before the start of the demolition was announced our landlord advised us that the developers were offering a payout to all store owners. We were given two choices, accept compensation for our business, the amount of which we did not know, or accept the landlord's offer to move to an empty store that she had available at the time. This was not something we wanted to do. We had spent a considerable amount of money to transform the store to a deli restaurant. It was only about four years that we had opened the business. Also, we had a significant amount of equipment that we had purchased to put in the store.

Setting up this store called for a major overhaul of everything that was in it. And since we had no intention of setting up the business in another location, we made the decision to complete the rest of our lease which was less than a year to go. Once our landlord made the decision to sell the complex with all the stores that she owned, we decided that we would either sell the business to someone who might be willing to accept the offer of setting up at another location when the developer was ready to demolish the complex or selling our equipment.

After mulling over what our next move should be, we discussed the matter with our lawyer. While no logically thinking person would want to invest in a business that was about to be eliminated by Eminent Domain, there was this one buyer who was willing to take a chance in doing just that. The landlord could not allow that to happen since she no longer had the power to lease the store to anyone. Locating to another spot was out of the question because it would involve a substantial sum of money, which would amount to much more than the pay-out we would get from the developers who were about to take over the complex.

We decided that it would be best to auction off all the equipment in the restaurant. To this end we contacted an auctioneer we heard about in New York City to discuss selling all the equipment in the store. He advised us about how an auction works, approximately how much we can expect for all the equipment, based on its value at the time. We felt somewhat frustrated over the whole ordeal and just wanted to get the process done as quickly as possible. After agreeing to go ahead with an auction, a date was set for the sale of the equipment.

Prior to the auction, the owners of a large mall that was just a few blocks from where our store was, came to us and asked us if we would be willing to relocate our business to that mall. While it was some food for thought, we turned down the offer because we would not have had control over what hours our days of the week we can open or close. It would be a 9a.m. to 10 p.m. routine seven days a week. Furthermore, at our ages at that time we would have been looking to completely burn out ourselves. Subsequently we turned down the offer and continued with the preparation for the auction.

There were several restaurant owners who came to the auction. Many of them looking for a good bargain on equipment. All our equipment was still relatively new since we were in the food business just about four and a half years at the time. Although we did not get as much as we hoped to for all the equipment plus we had to pay the auctioneer for setting up the auction, we believe that we had made the right decision to auction off all the equipment at that time rather than going through another expensive hassle to set up somewhere else. Besides, we were now approaching regular retirement age and it would not have made sense for us to set up the business elsewhere.

Finally Time for a Real Vacation

As in our first venture, there were those loyal customers whom we missed. But like everything in life, all things must come to an end. After the close of Tropical Isles, we decided that it was time for us to take that vacation we often talked about but never made the effort to make it happen. Now after fifteen years of dedicating most of our time to Flick City video store and Tropical Isles Gourmet Deli we were finally able to take a trip to Bermuda have a few dips in the ocean and relax.

After our Bermuda vacation we got bit by the travel bug. Subsequently, we joined a senior travel group and took some bus trips to various scenic areas along the eastern part of the USA. Once we had enjoyed ourselves by taking advantage of all the things we were missing out on for several years, we were so relaxed that it was almost like we should be doing something. To fill this feeling of void we got more involved in our neighborhood activities. Our community association was inactive for some years because of lack of member involvement.

Victor ran for President of our neighborhood association. He attended several meetings to discuss various aspects of improvement for the community. He designed and printed a community booklet for neighborhood watch program as well as printing the association's monthly newsletter.

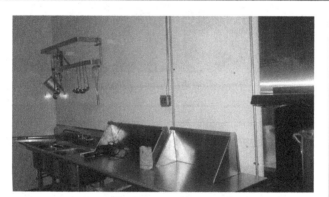

Installed kitchen equipment

Installed kitchen equipment

Installed Kitchen equipment at Tropical Isles Deli

Installed kitchen equipment

Installed kitchen equipment

Customers Dining in at Tropical Isles Deli

CHAPTER 13

⁂

Real Estate –
The Third Venture

After the terrorist attack in New York City on September 11, 2001 the stock market reacted with a severe drop as 401ks, and investors' portfolios took a punishing hit. Some investments were completely wiped out as the market spiraled on a downward trend for several months. This unfortunate situation hastened a housing bubble and an avalanche of foreclosures as several banks and mortgage companies foreclosed on properties because many of the owners were unable to maintain their mortgages.

This calamity provided an opportunity for some investors to invest in the housing industry during that time. Realtors were on the prowl for investors who wanted to seize the opportunity to benefit from the foreclosures. The real estate market was flooded with an overwhelming number of properties that succumbed to the housing bubble and the recession that followed.

Investors were taking advantage of the opportunity to purchase one or more of these properties since they were going for unbelievably low prices. Depending on an investor's credit rating, no down payment was required to purchase one of these foreclosed properties. Although we were now fully retired and was doing more traveling than we had done in many years we could not resist the temptation to invest in one of these properties. Our son bought one of these foreclosed properties and he encouraged us to take advantage of the opportunity to do likewise since we would not have to outlay any funding to purchase one of them. Getting into the rental property business would be another venture for us. Even though we had heard negative stories that some landlords experience with rental situations that were not good we decided to purchase one of the foreclosures anyway.

We were visiting our son who had now been settled in his aviation career in Atlanta, Georgia. During that visit we were introduced to a realtor who walked us through the procedure of looking for an ideal rental property. One that would be near to amenities such as grocery store shopping, and medical facilities.

Once we went through the routine of what to expect in getting one of these properties, it all sounded enticing. When it came time to go out with the realtor to look for a property, we were amazed at the number of foreclosures that were advertised on many of the streets in Atlanta, Georgia. At times we felt sorry for all the owners who had to lose their properties because of the recession. We had to consider ourselves among the lucky ones who were not in that predicament at the time.

The first day we went out with the realtor we saw four nice properties. Two of them were in locations that would be too far away for a renter who may not have some means of adequate transportation to get to a grocery or for other shopping.

One of the properties we saw that day had the attic stairway partially ripped apart from the ceiling and large gashes in the woodwork of the floor. The agent apologized for showing us that one. She said that this was the first time she had seen the inside of the house. She also said that some homeowners got angry when their properties were foreclosed on. Occasionally they would thrash parts of the property in retaliation for the predicament they were experiencing.

We were shown at least half a dozen properties that were for sale. We also witnessed what an eviction looked like once a tenant was put out of a property – furnishings, clothing put on the street corner waiting to be either picked up by garbage collectors or rummaged through by people looking to see what valuable items they could get from the evicted tenant. We had never seen so many properties in one area with foreclosed signs.

Our search went on for about two months before we finally settled for an attractive four-bedroom brick bungalow. This property was located near a major shopping mall with a Macy's Department Store and some other smaller clothing and sneaker stores. There were some eateries and a large family type restaurant located in the mall. Outside the mall was a medical facility, grocery stores, two banks and a day care center.

The bungalow was priced at an unbelievably low price. Once we went over all the particulars with the realtor who showed us the property the sales agreement was drawn up, and the next step was to get an approval for a mortgage. Finally, all documents were executed. Our next challenge was to get the house rental ready. For this we were introduced to a licensed plumber, a carpenter an electrician and a painter that we could use for any repairs, etc. that had to be done to the property.

With an abundance of facilities, including easy access to mass transportation and banking facilities, it was a perfect location for a renter. Our son also joined in the investment market purchasing a total of three foreclosed properties in the period between 2006 and 2010. As we were about to find out, this venture would be more of a headache than was worth the effort because it involved having direct dealings with a variety of personalities with varying living habits.

CHAPTER 14

※※※

Tenant No. 1

It was now January 2006 when we advertised our bungalow for the first renter. This ad was placed in the local paper. In about one week after it was listed, at least twenty people responded. After interviewing the first six people over the phone we settled for a family consisting of a grandmother, two daughters and a granddaughter. This family was displaced from their home in New Orleans due to Hurricane Katrina in 2005. The grandmother, who was responsible for renting the property, was screened and a lease was signed for twelve months. She was given a list of things that were expected of them as far as keeping the property in the same condition they found it barring normal wear and tear. The family members were all excited to finally get a decent place of abode, after the harrowing experience of living in a residential hotel for six months after the hurricane had ravished their home in New Orleans.

This tenant paid her rent on the due date for eight months (February through September 2006.) At the beginning of October, she notified us that she would be moving at the end of the month because one of her daughters had to commute from on Fridays from New Orleans to Atlanta and she was getting tired of the routine.

We told her we understood her situation and reminded her that the lease was for twelve months February 1,2006 to January 31, 2007. We also reminded her that, according to the terms of her signed lease. she will lose the deposit if she breaks the lease. She told us that there was an announcement from President Bush stating that victims of hurricane Katrina can break a contract before the lease ends.

We believed that she probably got her house in New Orleans repaired and did not want to let us know. It would have been more appropriate if she asked for a six-month lease, under the circumstances, and then ask for an extension. We allowed her to break the lease without forfeiting her deposit.

From this our first real estate experience we got an idea of what to expect from the world of landlord- tenant dealings. That it would be fraught with unforeseen situations that would require the patience of Job. Looking back on this our first endeavor in the Landlord-Tenant experience, we felt that although it was not a pleasant one, it was a necessary one to help prepare us somewhat, for what we would have to deal with as we move further along with this venture. We realized at that point that our endurance would be tested and our ability to tolerate the nuances that we were about to encounter in the landlord-tenant journey.

After this unfortunate experience, it was recommended that we should register the house with the Atlanta Housing Authority program which assists families in finding and paying for housing that they would otherwise not be able to afford. The Agency's rules and regulations are strict with guidelines that provide landlords with protection from circumstances such as broken leases, and guaranty landlords that their rents will be on time every month once the property meets the Housing Authority standard for approved properties. The rules also protect the tenants with rights for themselves such as not paying their portion of rent because of situations they may encounter such as hurricanes, tornadoes, floods or acts of nature. It seems that mostly women who are the caretakers of their households, especially with young children are the greater beneficiaries of this program.

CHAPTER 15

·※※※·

Tenant No. 2

After the first tenant finally moved out of our rental property, we had to prepare our place again before we could offer the house for rent to another prospective tenant. After going through the motion of preparing the property for another renter, we placed another ad outlining the details of the property such as size of the house, and the monthly rent. This time we had close to fifty responses since we let it run in the paper for a full two weeks. Eventually, we selected five prospective tenants to be interviewed. While none of them had a perfect rental history, we settled on a husband and wife who, at least, had a job. After a background check, we decided to rent them the property.

A twelve-month lease was prepared for their perusal and signature. In the lease, we underscored the part that said no pets were allowed on the property. Additionally, the lease stated that they could renew the lease at the end of the twelve months once the premises remained in the same condition it was rented to them, barring normal wear and tear. Everything was fine for the first six months or so, even though the rent was sometimes four or five days late. In our lease we allowed a grace period of about five days.

After being in the house for roughly ten months they began to pay the rent later and later. The excuse for the late payment was that the wife was sick, or the husband did not get enough hours on the job. We had expenses such as mortgage, insurance, taxes, etc. and could not allow this behavior to go on any longer. It was only after we threatened them with eviction that we were able to get them to move out voluntarily. When we finally were able to get them to move out of the house the amount of rent owed us was for more than three months. We were never able to collect the rent from them because they were nomadic.

While investing in real estate can be financially rewarding. we could never have imagined that the road to achieving financial success in the rental property arena would be paved with the difficulties we encountered when we decided to invest in what we believed was a fantastic real estate deal. While our first tenant may have had a legitimate reason for violating the terms of her lease agreement, her rent payments were on time and sometimes she even paid before the actual due date.

After the second negative experience, we decided to inquire further about the Housing Authority Section 8 program as a source for selecting prospective tenants. Our first step in this direction was to attend one of the Authority's meetings so that we could learn more about the rules and regulations of the program and the obligations of a landlord-tenant lease agreement.

At this meeting we learned that the Authority had a long waiting list of prospective tenants who were hoping for a call that a house was available for them to rent. Many of the Authority's recipients were young single mothers with between three and five young children. At the completion of the landlord-tenant meeting we were given a handbook with some literature that fully explained the rules and regulations of the Authority's program.

Our next step was a separate meeting with one of the Authority's counselors who answered any questions we needed to have further clarified about a landlord versus a tenant's obligations in the execution of a lease. We signed up for the program with the hope that this route would yield a reliable tenant that would adhere to the terms of a lease.

Soon after our meeting with the counselor we placed an advertisement in the local paper, giving a full description of the house (a spacious four-bedroom all brick bungalow with two- and one-half bathrooms, kitchen, living room and a large den.) The ad was listed in the newspaper for two weeks. On the second day it was listed we received several calls from people interested in renting the house Most of the responders were recipients of the Housing Authority's Section 8 program.

CHAPTER 16

·※※·

Tenant No. 3

This tenant was one of the first people to respond to the ad that we placed in the paper. After an introductory phone call an in-person interview was set up for her to come to see the house. When we did the walk through to show her all the rooms and the large backyard and front lawn, she expressed excitement by telling us that this house was perfect for her and her five kids. She said that she had passed by the house before when it was empty and was happy that it had finally become available for rent. She said that she desperately needed a larger place for her family (two teenage girls and three boys (ages 6 through 10).

Finding a four-bedroom house for rent was a stretch since most rentals that were advertised at that time had only three bedrooms. We questioned her in conjunction with some personal details about where she worked and why she wanted to leave the place she was living at the time. She told us that she was a nurses' aide and that her rent was being subsidized by the Housing Authority because she was a single mom and could not afford to pay for a place without some assistance.

We were relatively new in the landlord-tenant arena and not fully prepared to query her extensively about her living conditions at that time. Our assumption was that since she was a Housing Authority recipient with an approved Section 8 voucher that automatically qualified her as someone that would take care of our house if we rented it to her. The Housing Authority program had strict rules and regulations that all tenants had to meet to qualify for a housing voucher.

That stipulation reinforced our belief that we were on the right track when we accepted her as a tenant without significant scrutiny. After interrogating her as much as we could we gave her a rental application which she immediately filled out and gave us the required security deposit and application fee. We told her that we will call her once we reviewed the application, checked her credit, proof of employment, and contact her current landlord for a reference.

After calling the telephone number she gave us at least seven times, to inquire about her rental status at that address we got no response leaving a message each time. About a week or so we contacted her to let her know that we could not get a response from her current landlord, and we wanted to know if the number she gave us was correct. She verified that the number was the correct one. She said that the landlord may be out of town on a holiday or on a business trip. When we could not get a response from the landlord that should have been a clue that something was amiss.

Perhaps the landlord did not like the idea of giving references to anyone calling on the phone, as opposed to someone submitting a request for a reference in writing. However, since she was a Housing Authority participant with a valid Section 8 voucher, we decided to give her the benefit of the doubt. And after discussing with her what we expected from her as a tenant, we had a twelve-month lease drawn up for her perusal.

The lease clearly stipulated what we expected from her as a tenant "pay her portion of the rent on time; keep the house clean and tidy; she would be responsible for any damage to the property, barring any normal wear and tear." Additionally, there was a clause in the lease advising her that she should consider taking out a renter's insurance policy in case of any unforeseen loss to her property. The lease also specified that only she and her five children (named by age and sex) should be living in the house which meant no subletting. No pets were allowed! She said that she fully understood the "Terms of Agreement" of the lease. She signed the lease, gave us her one month's deposit plus her portion of the rent for that first month. Once her utilities were scheduled for her move in date, we gave her the keys and met her at the house on the move-in day to do a walk through, take pictures of all areas of the house and check that all utilities were in working order. While she was moving in three of her younger kids started to run up and down the stairs. We became a little concerned when her sons started to slide down the rail of stairs.

Our naivete placed us in line for one of the biggest mistakes we made in our Real Estate business venture. Regrettably, one thing we did not do before renting the house to her was to pass by the house where she was currently living. If we had done so we could have gotten a better idea as to how she would keep our place which would have been a big clue for us not to rent the house to her. A Housing Authority stipulation is that a landlord should visit the residence to observe the living habits of a prospective tenant. Such observation would be a tremendous help to the prospective landlord in making the right decision about renting a participant. While we did not do the maximum scrutiny of this tenant, everything seemed alright during the first six months of her tenantry.

As we were out of town several times during the first rental year for this tenant, we had our son, who was available at that time, visit the property. About three months after she had moved in, we called her to let her know that he would stop by to see how everything was going at the property.

The day he visited the house he observed that she had an oversized washing machine forcibly placed in the washroom. She said that she had leased the machine from a company which leases washing machines and dryers to renters. However, the machine could not fit in the washroom which also housed the water heater. Instead of calling us for advice as to what she should do, she let the delivery people force the machine to fit in the space causing damage to the door and the walls in that area.

Once a year the Housing Authority inspects a property that is participating in their Housing Choice program. A landlord is expected to see that the property is maintained in accordance with the standards set forth by the Housing Authority. The inspector will look to see that the following items are in order:

- Smoke detectors are working
- Fire extinguisher is filled with chemical for extinguishing a fire
- Water temperature is adequate

- Check the A/C to ascertain there are no leaks
- Electrical outlets are all intact
- Windows and doors in the house can open and close properly
- Screens on doors and windows are properly affixed and not torn
- No visible indication of roaches in the house
- Lawn is properly upkept
- Garbage is not scattered around the property
- House number is visible on mailbox

If any of the inspection issues are not up to standard the owner will be issued a failed report and the rental payment will be withheld from the landlord for up to thirty days until the discrepancies are resolved.

Our first Housing Authority annual inspection revealed that the following items were damaged resulting in a failed report on the property:

- Loose covers on several outlets
- Broken wall sockets

These broken items were the result of the tenant's carelessness and disregard in the handling of the washing machine. After we got the issues corrected the house was reinspected and finally received a "pass". Soon after the issues were resolved we paid another visit to the property to see if there were any other issues occurring in the washroom area. During that visit, we observed another occupant in the house who was not on the lease. When we inquired if she did indeed add another person to the household who was not on the lease, she replied that she did. She said that he was her nephew and that he was staying with her temporarily. We reminded her that her lease could be terminated because of this and that she should make sure that the nephew's current occupancy is terminated as soon as possible. She said that she would comply.

This kid had a dispute with another kid at school and, at some point, a fight broke out between them. One day the kid came to the house seeking revenge. He threw a rock at the house, breaking one of the windows. She called us to let us know about the incident. We were out of town at the time and asked our son to go to the house to find out what was going on. He was on an assignment for his job and could not get there in time to assess the damage. When we finally got there a week later, we discovered that there was a large hole in the pane of one of the windows. When we asked her about what happened she said that she was sorry and lamented that she was unable to control her kids. We could have asked her to leave at that time. However, we felt sorry for her and gave her one more chance to stay in the house at that time, but with a warning that if there were any other incidents, we would have to ask her to leave.

After making several inquiries about where we could find a place that repairs windows, we found a company to replace the window and told her that she must pay for the cost of the repair. She said that she did not have the means to pay for the repair. At this point we realized that the landlord-tenant relationship was imperiled by these incidents that occurred so early in the time that she occupied house, and it was obvious that things were not going to work as well as we hoped.

We admonished her that it was imperative that she have some control of her household if she wanted to continue to live in our property. She apologized and said that she understood the importance of having a nice house to live in and that she would make every effort to tackle the issue of getting full control of her household. We called her once a week to find out how everything was going for her. Even though it was her responsibility to have the lawn cut during the summer months we hired a landscaper to cut the grass monthly and to clear the leaves during the fall.

During her third year in the house another incident occurred. This time she had no choice but to quickly notify us since the incident involved a fire in the kitchen. We got to the house as soon as we could We were shocked at the scene we saw in the kitchen.

- The stove top grill was burnt.
- The kitchen and dining room walls were black with smoke.
- The cabinets were black and greasy.
- The ceiling fan was filled with grease.

When we asked what happened she said that while she was at work her oldest daughter invited some of her friends over to the house to watch a program on T.V. While they were all in the bedroom on the second floor her daughter left a pot with something on the stove for an unknown amount of time. Eventually, the pot boiled over, causing a fire in the kitchen. The flames from the unattended pot started to spark, filling the air with dense smoke and grease. All we could think of is what if the whole house had been burned down. The time had come for us to take more drastic measures with this tenant to safeguard the property. We told her that she should think about looking for another place to live. She begged us not to put her out, lamenting once again the difficulty she had in controlling her children. She told us that her uncle would help her clean up the smoke and grease that was on the walls and ceiling in the kitchen and dining areas.

November that year was once again time for the annual inspection by the Housing Authority. We requested that the inspection be done in December since we had two doctor's appointments in November. They said it was not necessary for the property owner to be present for the inspection if the head of household (the Housing Authority participant) was there. This time when the house was inspected it received a failed report outlining the below listed items as reasons for the failure:

Issue #1

A broken ceiling fan in one of the bedrooms occupied by her sons. Apparently one of her sons was using the ceiling fan for either a "Tarzan or Superman" stunt. The fan was almost completely torn from the ceiling. It created a sizeable hole and cracked the ceiling in several areas.

Issue #2

The house had become heavily infested with roaches. They were in the cabinets and the drawers. Even the bedroom closets and bathrooms had roaches crawling in them.

Issue #3

The door to the den had a large hole punched in it. When we eventually got to the house to assess the situation, it was an unbelievable sight to behold. It seemed like one million roaches had overtaken the place. We had to set off about eighteen bombs to try to get rid of some of the roaches. Additionally, we had to hire a pest control company to finally get rid of the roaches.

Besides the roach scenario, she had someone put a basketball hoop on the front lawn and another in the driveway so that her sons and their friends could play basketball whenever they wanted to. They used the front lawn of the house as a basketball court. While we were outside assessing the damage done to the lawn which had become bare of any visible grass, a neighbor saw us and said that she was glad that we came to see how the tenant was letting her children destroy our property as well as bringing down the neighborhood. She said this scenario would go on every evening after the kids came home from school, and sometimes on the weekends. The lawn had become so trampled and battered, that there was not even a blade of grass left on it. Only the clay soil was visible.

CHAPTER 17

·❀·❀·❀·

The Eviction

The time had come for us to evict this tenant. She and her children were destroying our property. We sent her a letter giving her thirty days to leave the house or be evicted. When our son went to the house to hand deliver the letter to her one of her young sons came to answer the door. He said to his mother "a man is at the door, do you want me to beat him up". She eventually came to the door and our son gave her the letter. After reading the letter she called us to say that she did not want to move. We had made up our minds that she had to be evicted.

The Housing Authority was notified of our decision to have her evicted. She, of course, tried to make excuses for not wanting to leave. After she realized that her excuses were not going to work with us this time, she wanted us to give her six weeks to leave. Meanwhile, the Housing Authority had given us thirty days to have the damages fixed or we could be removed from their program. Eventually, we filed a notice in the court to have her evicted. The court acknowledged receipt of the eviction request and a marshall was sent to the house to post the notice which stated that if she did not leave the property in two weeks, she was to appear in court on a specific date for an eviction hearing.

On the day she appeared in court she again lamented that she was unable to control her kids. She said that we did not give her a chance to rectify anything. At the eviction hearing the full cost of the damage to our property was presented to the court. She was ordered to pay the full cost of all the damage. Additionally, she was given seven days to remove all her belongings from our property or they would be. thrown out on the sidewalk. It was unbelievable that she did not leave the house after the seven-day deadline.

Our son, who was designated to take care of the eviction called the court to let them know that she was ignoring the court judgment. Eventually a marshall came to the house with a crew to remove her belongings from the house. They took everything out of the house and put it all on the sidewalk as is the usual custom in the state of Georgia. She had no choice then but to leave.

Before leaving the house, she backed her car into the wrought iron rail at the side of the carport, severely damaging it. Also, one of her sons scrawled profanity on the side of the house. She never paid us the money that the court ordered her to pay us. Instead, she filed bankruptcy and we were unable to collect any of the payment that was due us.

We submitted a copy of her eviction to the Housing Authority. She was subsequently dropped from the Authority's Assistance program. After a while we became so frustrated with the whole situation, we did not even bother to pursue getting the judgment the court imposed on her. We felt it probably would have cost us more than it was worth to further pursue it. The main thing is that the Housing Authority did not remove our property from their listing. We got the pay for the month that was held back because of the last failed inspection.

After that eviction experience, we had the daunting task of the repairs that had to be done to restore our property to the condition it was in before this tenant occupied it. Below is a list of the repairs that had to done:

- Fix several large ceiling cracks throughout the house
- Replace broken fans in two bedrooms.
- Replace four damaged closet doors.
- Replace screen door at the entrance.

- Replace several blinds that were broken throughout the house.
- Paint all the walls
- Repair and paint all cabinet doors in the kitchen and replace all knobs
- Have all the carpeted areas in the house cleaned.
- Replace broken outlet covers throughout the house
- Repair significant damage to the washroom walls and floor
- Remove graffiti from the side of the house
- Fix the wrought iron rail in the carport
- Lay rolls of sod to repair the damaged front lawn

In addition to the repairs that had to be done to the property we had to let off several bombs to try to eliminate the infestation of roaches that this tenant left behind. With all the roach spraying that was done, we still had to hire a professional pest prevention company to return the house to a livable condition. It was three months before all the repairs could be completed. In the end, all the repairs, painting and general restoration of this property cost us roughly $16,500.

This tenant's security deposit was not enough to pay a fraction of what it costs us to repair the house and bring it back to a decent living standard. After the repairs were completed, we did not want to rent it again. It was that incident that made us realize that perhaps we should have avoided pursuing this venture since we were already at full retirement age.

CHAPTER 18

***

A Recession Sets In

It was now 2010 and the country was in a recession. We were pondering the best course of action to take after the awful experience we had with Tenant No. 3. We felt that perhaps we should sell the property. Upon checking the value of the property, we discovered that it had dropped significantly due to the recession. Selling the property at that time would have resulted in a significant financial loss to us. Subsequently we decided to weather the recession storm and hope for a quick rebound of the real estate market. One thing was for sure – there was a big demand for rental properties. We decided to rent the house at least one more time until the recession eases and property values hopefully increase.

At one of our family meetings, we acknowledged the fact that each misstep along the path to success is a lesson learned on how best to navigate the broken path. Our four-bedroom house was perfect for a family of four or five, especially since it had a large den which a family could utilize as an additional bedroom. The Housing Authority had a long list of families waiting for the opportunity to lease this type of house. After giving much thought about what was the best course of action to take, we said that we would rent it one more time.

At that point though we knew that we had to think about the steps we would have to take to avoid renting to the type of tenant we had to evict. To strengthen our resolve to stay the course we met with a Housing Authority landlord advisor to discuss the experience we had with the evicted tenant and what additional steps we should take when interviewing a future applicant. Some of the most significant takeaways we gleaned from the meeting with this Advisor were the following:

- After an initial phone interview and before accepting an application from a prospective tenant request a specific time to visit the current residence.
- Observe the cleanliness of the house
- Is the furniture tidy?
- Are there broken venetian blinds in the windows.
- Are they any animals in the house (i e. cats or dogs)

- Does the house smell as if it needs cleaning?
- Carefully observe the kitchen area since this is the busiest area in the house.
- Is there trash in the kitchen that looks like it should be taken out.
- Is the lawn overgrown?
- Are the leaves raked during the fall?
- Observe the behavior of the children – are they running around or are they well mannered.

We were told that a Housing Authority participant should allow a prospective landlord to observe the above listed things at the participant's current home of abode. If the prospective tenant seems reluctant to allow a prospective landlord to observe at least some of the key issues above, then that would be an indication as to what the landlord might expect from the tenant as far as upkeeping the property and having control of her household. Had we done an extensive interview of the tenant we had to evict, incorporating all the above issues. we would have avoided the damage to our property and subsequently the costly repairs that had to be done.

About two years after Tenant No.3 was evicted from our house, we saw her on a Court TV program on national Television and could not believe what we were seeing and hearing.

A plaintiff had brought a case against her for damages that one of her sons and another young boy did to the plaintiff's car. The man said that while his car was parked in his driveway sometime in the summer of that year, her son and his friend lit a napkin and threw the burning napkin through the car window of the plaintiff's car. The lit napkin landed on the back seat of the man's car and burned much of the upholstery on the car seat. The whole car could have been destroyed by the incident.

When the judge admonished them about the incident, they were just giggling. The only thing the mother could say is what we had heard her say quite often while she was a tenant in our house: "I'm unable to control my children." She had to pay the man for the damage her son and his friend had done to his car. A full $5,000 penalty which was the maximum allowed through the court. It was like witnessing Poetic Justice.

We decided to put the house up for rent again, so we placed the usual ad in the newspaper. Within one day of the ad being out in the paper, we got about fifty calls from people wanting to rent the house. Ninety percent of those responding to the ad were young women with about three to six young children. Some of them were the head of household in the family. They were all single moms and many of them were Housing Authority participants. Given our last experience with the mom of five children, we decided we would not consider anyone with more than three kids. Subsequently, we selected three callers for interviews at different times.

THE FIRST AT-HOME INTERVIEW

This interview was with a young woman with three young children. We made an appointment to meet her at the apartment where she was living. She agreed to have us come to her apartment for the interview and to observe how the apartment was being kept. We did not feel comfortable going to an apartment in an area that we did not know. However, it was something we had to do if we hoped to avoid problems like what we had with our third tenant. When we got to her apartment for the interview a young man holding a child met us at the front door. The applicant quickly came behind him and she ushered us in. She told us that the young man was her boyfriend and the father of the child he was holding. He was polite and we felt more at ease.

During the interview we asked her why she wanted to leave where she was living. She said that she wanted to move into a house with a backyard where her children would have more room to play. She also said that the apartment complex she was living in was not very safe for her and her children. We then got to the part of doing a walk through her apartment so that we could observe how the living quarters were kept especially the kitchen and bathroom areas. While the apartment was somewhat decent, we observed a couple broken blinds in the bedrooms. When we opened the closets, there were two cats in one of the closets. The odor was far from pleasant.

Our ad specified no pets would be allowed in our house. Perhaps she put the cats in the closet so that we could not see them right away. Our observations from this visit disqualified her as a tenant for us. We could not take the chance of repeating a mistake like the one we had with the previous tenant. We called her a couple days later to let her know that we had made the decision that we would be unable to use her as a tenant.

THE SECOND AT-HOME INTERVIEW

Our next interview was with a young lady who also had three children, one boy and two girls. Her reason for wanting to move was the usual, she needed more room for her family. Upon visiting her for the initial interview we immediately observed that the house was well kept and that her children were well behaved. The interview with her was favorable and, as far as we could see, she did not have pets around the house. The only drawback in this interview was that she had a large trampoline in the backyard. We asked her if she was going to bring the trampoline with her should we consider her as a tenant. Her response was that she would because her children would not want to give it up. We told her we would let her know our decision in a couple days.

Before making a final decision about whether to consider her as a possible tenant, we decided to do some research on reports we heard about backyard trampoline accidents. Our findings were that there were some incidents where some young children were injured from playing on backyard trampolines. We decided at that point that it would be unwise for us to have her as a tenant because she felt obligated to bring the trampoline with her for the sake of her children. We regretted that we had to notify her of our decision and explained to her that our homeowner's insurance would not cover for any possible injury that may occur from an accident on the trampoline.

It is sometimes difficult to make the decision when to rent or not to rent a prospective tenant. We have seen many prospects that would have been the ideal candidate for us to entrust our rental property to. We have learned along the way that like a rose, unless you know how to handle the thorns the prick could prove to be unforgettable anguish. With every unforeseen challenge we have encountered in the rental business, we have learned valuable lessons that have not only catapulted us into a higher realm of experience, but also sharpened our senses with keen observation as to whether a renter is for real or perhaps trying to outsmart us. We experienced the attempt by another renter who tried to play us with tricks that we could not have imagined had we not encountered just about everything there is to endure in the home rental business.

CHAPTER 19

·木木木·

Tenant No. 4

The next tenant that we put in our house was a perfect example of wit and cunning. She was one of several people who answered the ad we placed in the newspaper. Like most of the callers, she was a housing authority Section 8 recipient with a family which consisted of one boy 13 years old and two girls 16 and 17 years old. Even though a tenant should not have more people in the household than those listed in the lease, this rule is often ignored.

At this stage of the game, however, we were fully in sync with the stipulation that a landlord should pay a visit to where a prospective tenant is residing to observe the family structure, existing living conditions, how the property is kept both inside and outside, mannerisms of family members, and willingness to allow a prospective landlord to carefully observe areas, especially of the kitchen and lawn areas.

Our appointment with this prospective tenant was welcomed. She understood why we wanted to visit her place before we made the decision to rent her our house. We observed that there was a stack of boxes at the entrance to the house as though she had started to pack for a move. While doing our walk through, we observed that there were two single beds in one of the bedrooms.

Without hesitation, she told us that her daughters were now 16 and 18 and they wanted to have individual bedrooms. Throughout the house the rooms all looked relatively neat. The kitchen was very tidy—no garbage lying around. When we looked in the backyard, there was a high pile of leaves that seemed to have been there for a long time.

At the time of our visit her boyfriend was there. She told us that he was the father of her son and that he came to visit him that evening. We had no problem with that. Our main concern was how she kept her place. While we prefer to have all family members at home during our visit so that we could observe and detect behavior, only one daughter was at home at the time of our visit. She told us that the other daughter was at school taking extra classes because she would soon be graduating from high school. She added that the daughter recently was pregnant and was taking extra classes so she could graduate.

After giving much thought about what we observed during our visit to her home, we decided to rent her the house. When we called to let her know that we had made the decision to rent her the house she was excited.

We emailed her the application which she filled out promptly. Soon after she returned the completed application with the required fee of $25 so we could start the process of checking her background. There were some questionable issues in her profile such as collections, she explained that these collections were mostly for medical bills which at that time were resolved. After she completed the application form that is required prior to the final decision we completed some landlord forms that were required by the Housing Authority.

Once all forms were completed and verified, they were approved by the Housing Authority. The next thing was preparing a twelve-month lease for her. We advised her to carefully read the lease, and to pay special attention to the "Terms of Agreement" before signing the lease. After reading the lease she signed it. On her move in we did the usual walk through with her and took pictures of every room in the house. We also checked the utilities. Everything was working in perfect order. Once everything checked out okay, she was ready to complete the move in.

As usual, during the first year, everything went as well as could be expected. No issues with tidiness in the house; no roaches. We contracted a pest control company to treat the house four times a year (quarterly) for the purpose of adequate pest prevention. While it is the tenant's responsibility to have the lawn upkept, we hired a landscaper to mow the lawn once a month, trim the hedges and remove the leaves during the fall season.

As we would learn from our past experiences there is no such thing as a perfect tenant. Some habits can be tolerated, while others are a definite "no, no." This tenant was now the fourth person in the house. As a Housing Authority Section 8 recipient she adhered to the rules and regulations stipulated by the Housing Authority. We noticed, however, that the guy who was with her when we first met her had apparently settled down in the house with her. Even though the lease stipulated who was supposed to be living in the house, we did not make a big fuss about it since the house was kept as tidy as possible, at least whenever we visited.

On one of our visits, in preparation for the Housing Authority's annual inspection, we observed that they were several empty soda cans placed in a pile in a corner of the backyard. When we questioned the reason for the pile, she said that her guy was a collector of bottles and cans and that he would put them in a pile in the yard until he had a certain amount to redeem at a redemption depot. This was unacceptable so we asked her to let him know that we could not allow this behavior and he should immediately refrain from putting a pile of cans and bottles in the yard. She complied.

While she was living in the house every Housing Authority inspection passed without a problem. Sometime in the third year of her lease, just when everything was going smoothly – no roach issues, etc., we got a call from the utility company where she had her electric account. They wanted to know if we had given her a new lease.

We thought this was a prank that someone was trying to play on us. But when the caller said that they were calling from the utility company I told them that we did not issue the tenant a new lease and asked what this was all about. They said that her daughter brought in a new lease to them, stating that we had given her mother a new lease.

After some questioning, we found out that the mother had several late payments due on the utility bill. The utility company was going to cut off the service. To avoid having the service disconnected her daughter took the first page of the lease that we gave her mother originally and put the mother's boyfriend name on it. They attached the last page of the lease that had our signature and tried to open a new account. This was unbelievable. We had to add this feat to our list of "new lessons learned from a tenant's book of tricks".

"Here we go again" was the first thought that came to mind. Was there anything else for us to experience! Her oldest daughter was now 20 years old, had one child and was pregnant with another. Like her mom, she applied for a Housing Authority voucher to get her own place. This situation meant that the tenant could no longer claim her daughter as a dependent, therefore the amount of her monthly allowance from the Housing Authority would be reduced. This change also meant she would now have to pay us the portion of the rent that normally would be paid by the Housing Authority for her daughter.

Once her Section 8 subsidy was reduced, she advised us that she was not able to pay the difference after her daughter moved out of the house. She asked us if we would take a lesser amount of rent monthly. We, of course said we could not. We also told her that she would have to find a smaller place since her daughter would no longer be living at the house. To our detriment we were sort of stuck in perpetual motion. We could not even put the property up for sale if we wanted to at that time, because of the severe drop in property values due to the continuing recession

She insisted that she did not want to move but we told her that we would not be able to accommodate her by taking rent that was already at a low monthly rate. Soon after her daughter moved out, we were advised by the Housing Authority that they would be paying us a lesser monthly amount because our tenant's family structure was now three, instead of four. We had no other choice then than to give her a thirty-day notice to find another place. When the thirty days had almost expired, she was still hesitating, stating that she could not find another house and she did not want to live in an apartment. We then had to let her know that if she did not try to find another place, we will have no other choice but to have her removed through the process of the court. She knew that an eviction would hamper her chances of getting another place in the future.

Eventually she found a house a few miles further from the city where our house was. Even though she did not want to move that far away, she had no choice. One day her new prospective landlord called us for a reference on her. We advised him that she kept our place clean and that the reason she was moving was because of the change in her family structure.

About two weeks had gone by and she still had not yet made any concrete effort to move out of our property. When we asked about when she will be leaving, she said that the new prospective landlord had decided not to rent his house to her because he saw her smoking and he did not want to rent his house to a smoker. We could understand his reasoning but as far as we know she never smoked in our house. She asked us for an additional two weeks to move but we said we could not accommodate her. She had to eventually put her things in storage until she could find a place that was affordable for her.

During our final walk through with her to observe if there were any drastic changes to the condition of the house, we observed some graffiti scrawled on one side of the wall in the den. She said that her grandchild who at the time was about three years old, had scrawled the markings on the wall. However, the markings appeared to be made by a teenager or young adult. In accordance with the terms of her lease agreement, she was responsible for any damage that was done in the house since she did not rent the house in that condition. We deducted what it cost to remove to the graffiti markings from her security deposit and mailed the balance to her via certified mail specifying the deducted amount.

CHAPTER 20

‒‒‒ ⋇⋇⋇ ‒‒‒

The Recession Continues ‒ Our Plans Change

The recession was still causing a rapid decline in property values, with no indication as to when the situation would end. As much as we wanted to get out of the market at that time, it was impossible to do so because of the tremendous financial loss we would have suffered. Subsequently, we had no choice but to continue to stay the course. During that time there was no shortage of renters so we, reluctantly, decided to put the property up for rent again. Rent would be guaranteed since ninety-nine percent of the families that were looking for a four-bedroom house was on the Housing Authority's list.

Anyone trying to buy a home during the recession would experience an almost insurmountable feat since getting a mortgage as a first-time buyer was difficult. Several realtors turned to getting homeowners who were saddled with a huge amount of mortgage debt and increasing depreciation of property values, to sell their properties via a short sale as a way of getting out of their mortgage debt. The way that would work is if a homeowner had an existing mortgage of $150,000 and the depreciated value of the property was $50,000, a realtor could plea bargain for a $50,000 payoff, essentially getting the homeowner off the hook for the full mortgage amount.

We were one of many homeowners who were approached about doing a short sale if we decided to consider this route instead of the rental route. Pursuing the short sale route was not something we wanted to do. Short sales can affect credit scores and put a mortgagee in a bad credit category. We decided instead to rent our property at least one more time until the punishing recession ease and property values rebound.

As property values continued to drop, some investors were taking advantage of the significantly low home prices by purchasing houses that were foreclosed on. These investors would do partial or full repairs on the foreclosures they purchased and then sell them for a substantial profit. This practice was common in 2010 through 2012 when the profitability margin was at its highest.

CHAPTER 21

Tenant No. 5

When we decided to rent our property one more time, the Housing Authority's subsidies to participants were significantly reduced. Our choices at that time were not the best – either sell the property for less than half of what we paid for it or keep it with the hope that the recession would soon fizzle and that home values would increase. We placed an ad once more to rent the house. This time we received over one hundred requests from Housing Authority participants who were on a long waiting list for a rental. As it was in previous demands, the top housing choice was a four-bedroom house in a safe neighborhood.

After interviewing three applicants on the phone, we set up an appointment to meet with a middle-aged grandmother who was the apparent breadwinner for her daughter and two grandchildren (a boy and a girl – ages 12 and 14 at the time). We never questioned why she instead of the children's mother was responsible for finding a home for them. One thing we discovered along this journey, is that it is almost impossible to get a reference from a prospective tenant regarding their relationship with a previous landlord. It may be that some tenants might have had one issue or another with a landlord and therefore may give wrong or incomplete information about their rental history.

We set up an appointment to meet with this applicant where she was living. We immediately observed that the house was well kept. Everything was in order, furniture, etc. The kitchen area was clean and, based on the artistic décor she had in the dining and living rooms, it was obvious that she paid special attention to detail in keeping her place looking prim and proper. Although we did not meet her daughter at that initial at-home appointment, we observed that her grandchildren were very polite and mannerly.

We discussed with her about the type of tenant we were looking for. Since she was a Housing Authority participant, we believed that she would respect and adhere to the rules and regulations of the Housing Authority as well as the terms of agreement that would be laid out in our lease if we decided to rent her our property. She said she understood our desire to have the right tenant, especially since she was at that time an occupant of the property of another landlord. When we asked her reason for wanting to leave where she was living, she said that she needed a larger place for her family of four. Additionally, the area she was living in had some issues with break-ins and she wanted to move to a safer neighborhood.

After we reviewed her application and checked her background information, everything that we needed to know came back satisfactory. Subsequently, we notified her that she was approved and that we would be drawing up a lease for her to sign with a copy to go to the Housing Authority. She said she wanted to move as soon as possible. We advised her she should give her current landlord at least thirty days' notice of her plan to move. She acknowledged this obligation and we arranged for her to get our lease so she could sign it promptly.

Once the lease was signed and she gave us her security deposit of one month's rent, she was ready for the walk through which included pictures taken of all the major things in the house. After she signed her lease, she said that she was happy to get out of the neighborhood she was living in at the time. We wondered how it must have been but never questioned the extent of her displeasure with the place she was living. Amazingly, like in the case of some other tenants, we never got to speak directly with her former landlord. Once she was fully settled in our house, she kept it immaculate. We had no problem getting her rent on time since it was paid by the Housing Authority. She seemed like the ideal tenant that a landlord would want to have.

About four years into her tenantry the first negative incident occurred at the house. One Saturday during the summertime she, her daughter and her grandchildren went shopping. Her grandson, who was about 13 years old at that time, used the bathroom in the den before they all left the house. From what we were told, he dropped something in the toilet bowl and tried to flush it down. Because he flushed too many times the flush tank valve did not completely cover the area causing the tank to overflow and a pool of water to accumulate in the bathroom and the surrounding areas. He never told his grandmother or his mother about what happened and when they all returned to the house from shopping there was a pool of water in the bathroom, family room and an adjoining bedroom. She called to let us know what happened.

It was Sunday and we were out of town at that time. We immediately called our plumber and asked him to go check to see what was going on. It was a couple hours before he could get there. He called us to tell us that there was about six inches of water in the den the bathroom and a bedroom on that level. He explained to us that after the kid flushed the toilet the flange was not properly positioned, causing the water to constantly run until it overflowed. He said we would have to get a restoration company to do the job of removing all the water since he did not have the necessary equipment to do it.

We called our insurance company to report the incident and they referred us to a restoration company to come to assess the damage. The restoration team went to the house about two or three days after. They had to pump several inches of water out of the area. When they finished all the walls, facia boards and electrical units in the area were damaged. The carpet was saturated with water and not reusable.

Once we got the assessment as to what it would cost to repair the damage and restore the room to the way it was before the cost was a staggering $4,500. This price included new carpeting, electrical outlets, new fascia boards and painting of the den and bathroom areas.

The experience had become too much to absorb at that moment. After we filled out the papers to okay the repairs to be done, we had to wait to get the final approval from our insurance company. They agreed to cover the cost of the damage, but we had to pay a deductible of $1,000 towards the cost of the repair. It took approximately one month for repairs to be done. Eventually, our home insurance rate went up due to the claim. The restoration company did a superb job in restoring the area.

The tenant was concerned about what we may do because of the incident. However, we had no plan to evict her because we acknowledged that accidents could happen and that it really was not her fault or carelessness that caused this situation to occur. We also acknowledged that there will always be some trials and tribulations a landlord may encounter in a landlord tenant relationship. This incident clearly pointed out to the tenant the importance of having renter's insurance in case of any unforeseen loss or damage to personal property. After the water issue, the tenant said she was being careful and that she would try to explain to her grandson how to be careful whenever he used the bathroom.

It was now five years that the tenant was living in the house. Everything was going smoothly as it was prior to the bathroom incident. At some point however, she let one of her granddaughters move into the house without our permission. When we eventually found out what was going on, she told us that she was just trying to help this granddaughter who had a newborn baby and that it would only be for a few weeks until she got a place for herself and her child.

This, of course did not sit well with us because based on previous experiences, we knew that once a tenant encourages someone who is not on the lease to live in the house for any amount of time it never works out the way they say it is intended to. Furthermore, once a tenant does this it is a violation of the terms of the lease. We advised her that her granddaughter would have to move as soon as possible. We also told her that she was in violation of the terms of her lease which would be cause for an eviction. That was something she did not want to happen. Consequently, she complied accordingly.

There are some tenant misdeeds that a landlord may miss. A tenant knows that a landlord cannot always be around to observe most of these misdeeds. That tenant would therefore get away with some things that are inconsistent with the terms of a lease for a long time. It was now the seventh year that this tenant was living at the property. It was during that year we noted some deterioration in the way the property was being kept. Specifically, during the summer, the tenant was entertaining some friends when she placed a table in the carport to have card parties which would, at times, be boisterous to the point where some neighbors complained.

Besides the card games, she would hang wet mats on the railing of the carport to dry. At that point we felt that we had had enough and decided to once more think about selling the property since the recession was winding down and housing prices and the demand for properties were increasing. It was now a good time for property sales.

It was 2019 and the market prices for houses were strong. We got a realtor to do a market analysis of the property values in the area. From the analysis it was determined that our house could sell for approximately three times more than it would have just two years prior to that date. The house was all brick and had a new roof put on it before the current tenant moved in. The kitchen was renovated after we evicted the tenant whose daughter caused a fire in it.

We were now ready to notify the current tenant that we were going to sell the house. We told her that we were selling the house and that she should start to look for another rental. We gave her sixty days to find a place. She said that she did not want to move and asked us if we could let her stay for another two years when her grandson would graduate. and she did not want him to leave the school he was in for several years. We told her we understood but we had to sell the house at that time. It did not seem that the child's mother, who was also living at the house played any significant role in the decision making for the young boy. That, of course, was not our business.

When the house was eventually placed on the market there was a slew of buyers who put in their bid for the property. Some of these potential buyers were investors looking to buy properties for as low as they could possibly get them. Their objective was to sell them for a higher price so they could make a large profit in record time. The first potential buyer the realtor brought to the house met significant resistance from the tenant. The realtor told us that the tenant had an attitude and was very harsh and somewhat abusive towards a junior realtor that took a client to view the house. She said the tenant would not allow the prospective purchaser to view all the rooms as is customary in a walk through. The tenant purposely kept the lights off in the bedrooms and called the realtor and the buyer "hoodlums."

This attitude on her part turned off the first prospective buyer. The tenant did everything possible to discourage a realtor from showing any prospective buyer the house. She even took down the "For Sale" sign that the realtor had place on the front lawn of the house. We could not let this sort of behavior continue so we decided to go to the house with the realtor and the next prospective buyer to avoid the previous encounter.

The second person that viewed the property liked it immediately and the ball was set in motion to draw up the necessary papers with the realtor for a sale agreement. Once everything checked out the buyer got her approval for a mortgage and the documents for a closing date were executed. When the house was eventually sold it was a big relief for us.

Renting this particular property was problematic because the occupants that were drawn to it were mostly young women who were participants of the Housing Authority Section 8 program. Unfortunately, some of them found it difficult to control their children's destructive behavior.

Listing the property in the Housing Authority's Section 8 program (it could accommodate a family of up to five people, and it had a large back and front yard which was a plus for a large family. Some renters did not appreciate this advantage and they let their kids ravish the property, costing us a significant amount of money in repairs. Additionally, these problem tenants disregarded the obligation they had to comply with the terms of the leases they signed before occupying the property. By doing so, they also disregarded the obligation they had of recognizing the Housing Authority's rules for participants of the program.

Four Bedroom Bungalow

CHAPTER 22

Tenant No. 6

During a period of eight years, our son acquired four of the foreclosed properties that saturated the market during the housing bubble and eventual recession. Of a total of fourteen tenants that rented his properties four of them had to be evicted, mostly for non-payment of rent. One of the properties, a quadruplex located near the largest and busiest airport in the country, had four generous sized one-bedroom apartments. Each of these apartments had a spacious bedroom, living room and a bonus room that could be used as a second bedroom or a dining room. The tenants that rented these apartments were mostly single professional women.

There was one tenant who could be considered as the perfect renter. She paid her rent on the due date every month. Her apartment had a balcony with a picturesque view of the city skyline. She kept the apartment immaculate and always decorated the balcony with beautiful plants and seasonal flowers. A landlord could not have asked for a more ideal tenant. Three years after she occupied the apartment, another apartment located below hers became vacant. She wanted to rent it for her elderly mother so that she could be closer to her. She said she would pay the rent and the electric bill for her mother. Without hesitation he agreed to rent her the apartment for her mom.

After the lease was signed, she arranged for a company to bring all the mother's belongings to the apartment. Since she worked during the day, she said that her brother who was unemployed at the time, would come to the apartment during the day to stay with their mother and attend to her needs until she got home from work. Then in the evening he would go back to his place. and she would take over the mother's care. This arrangement seemed to be going as planned. However, after the first few months her brother started to stay overnight and was not paying for additional utilities he was using as he had now moved in with the mother without a written consent. This situation caused a rift between the tenant and her brother. She then decided that she was not going to pay the electric bill anymore for the mother's apartment.

After two or three unpaid bills the utility company cut off its service leaving the apartment without electricity. Since the stove was all electric her mother was unable to do any cooking. Also, she had to use a candle to see at night because the apartment was in total darkness for some days.

This discord among them created a huge problem. One day another tenant called us to say that there was an alarm that was going off non-stop in the building and there was a smell of smoke coming from the mother's apartment. When our son went to the building to investigate the situation, he discovered that the tenant's brother had placed some material on the stove to try to cook something and it set off all the alarms in the building. He questioned his tenant about the incident and told her that she would have to pay for any damage that was done to the stove and the kitchen. She told him that it was her brother that was causing the problem, and she was unable to reason with him because she did not want to upset the mother.

In addition to all this disturbance, the mother invited some odd characters to picnic on the front lawn of the quadruplex during the daytime. They were eating Kentucky fried chicken and creating and indecent sight in the neighborhood. These characters would also drop empty food bags and napkins on the lawn. Our son told them that they were forbidden from utilizing his property as a park and advised the tenant that if she did not do something about forbidding her mother and her brother's parade of characters from bringing food on the lawn, he would have to evict both she and her mother. So now the once perfect tenant had created a problem by renting the apartment for her mother, paving the way for an even bigger problem for herself in the form of a potential eviction.

It was summertime and the mother and brother continued to encourage the parade of characters to congregate on the front lawn of the apartment building. Our son went to the court to file an eviction against the tenant and her mother. At the eviction hearing the judge gave them seven days to leave the premises or be removed by a marshall.

The mother and son eventually left. However, our son allowed her to keep her apartment because he realized that it was not her intention to create the mess that occurred because of her brother's influence on their elderly mother. Eventually, it was business as usual. The tenant remained in her apartment and her mother moved in with the brother and his girlfriend elsewhere.

Just a few months had gone by, and things did not go well for the mother and brother. The mother wanted to come back to live with her. She asked our son if it was possible for her to bring the mother back this time to live in the apartment with her. He told her it was not feasible since the mother was already evicted. He said that he would give her thirty days to find a place where she could be with her mom as she always wanted to. She eventually found a two-bedroom house to rent so that she could have her mom with her.

It was almost a year after she left when he received a call from her wanting to know if he had any apartments available for rent. His answer was no! He never found out what exactly was the reason she wanted to move from the house she had move to only a few months prior, but he could have only imagined that it was most likely a situation like the one he had to deal with while she was at his property.

Quadruplex rental property

CHAPTER 23

The Other Properties

Once we entered the rental property arena, we became aware of some complexities we had only heard about but could never fathom because we lacked the firsthand experience of dealing with the variety of personalities we eventually encountered. It was sometimes difficult to understand the thought process of those individuals who would sign a lease confirming that they understood what it meant to fulfill the obligations of the terms of a lease. Yet when the time came to adhere to rules and regulations of the signed document, it's like they are in different world.

Most of the tenants in these other properties were hard working adults who were appreciative of the houses they were renting. Our son owned these properties and we helped him manage them. He did not experience the magnitude of problems we had with the tenant that was evicted from our four-bedroom house. However, there was this one young lady who responded to an ad he placed in the local newspaper advertising a three-bedroom house he had for rent. After a phone interview she was given an appointment to come to view the house.

On the day of her in-person appointment he asked her why she wanted to move from where she was living at the time. She replied that she needed more room for her two young children whom she brought to the appointment with her. She was also asked the critical question about if she was ever evicted from an apartment or house. She replied "no"! He then gave her an application which she promptly filled out and paid the application fee of $25 She was told that she would be notified after her credit history and job references were checked. The report came back that her credit history was not good because she had a few overdue and outstanding bill payments. However, he acknowledged that sometimes people may fall on hard times and deserve a chance to redeem themselves.

She was notified of the discrepancies that may hinder her ability to pay the monthly rent when it was due. Nevertheless, he decided to give her a chance and eventually approved her for renting the house. She paid her first month's rent and one month deposit as required. A standard twelve-month lease was drawn up highlighting the terms of agreement. She was given a couple days to digest the requirements of the lease and what would be expected of her as a tenant. After the lease was signed the move-in date was set and on the day of her move-in he went over the check list of all the appliances, etc. that were in the house. The day she moved in the house everything seemed quite normal. She did not have an excessive amount of furniture and there was no indication that anything was amiss. She was all set in her new dwelling and she seemed quite excited and expressed that now her kids would have a yard to play in because she lived in an apartment before where the play area was limited.

It was now about three months after she settled in the house that things started to go in the wrong direction. She started to pay her rent late and he had to chase her down to get the rent which, on one occasion, she paid in single dollars. So much for giving a single mom a break! He could not have envisioned that in about six months into her lease this tenant would utilize the garage to conduct a side business. It seemed that she was involved in the rap music industry. What role she played in this business was unknown. However, at some point she allowed someone to construct a mini music studio in the garage and had several people who were involved in this type of music come to practice in the garage.

Several neighbors complained to him about the excessive noise that these people were keeping. When he went to investigate what was going on he discovered the structure that was built in the garage. Additionally, they were several empty beer cans that were on the lawn and in the driveway. He told her that he could not tolerate this behavior and that she had violated the lease terms. Also, she had caused damage to his property by having someone illegally construct a fixture in the garage of the property.

She was given two weeks to leave voluntarily, or he would have her evicted. He eventually had to take her to the court to get her out of the house. She left willingly so that he did not have to get a marshall to put her out.

SUMMARY

Our journey through these three business ventures has been one of excitement that was sometimes tinged with difficult encounters. Even though we entered the business arena not knowing if we would succeed, we were intent on proving that doing the right research into how to navigate the world of business, having the necessary capital to cover expenses beyond the six-month to one year start-up of business, recognizing the importance of effective advertising plus portraying good customer relationship are key factors in accomplishing success.

Along the way we learned some valuable lessons about dealing with customers. While location and a substantial market are critical factors for exposure of your business, the product and service provided to customers are of utmost importance. After all who would want to patronize a business where both the service and the products are of the lowest quality even if that business is right next door to where you reside. Dissatisfied customers could mean a loss to a business and subsequently a loss of the business. Throughout the journey especially in the businesses where we had direct contact with customers, we always strive to be helpful, and customers appreciated the attention we gave them.

While the rental property business can sometimes be rewarding there are those times when it can be so frustrating that even the calmest person would feel like it is a waste of time trying to cope with the nuances of some tenants with really bad habits. Most of the tenants who rented our four-bedroom house had Housing Authority Section 8 vouchers and large families. Even with their own sizeable families, some of them would ignore their lease obligations and allow other people who were not on the lease to come and live with them thus flaunting their disrespect for the landlord's efforts to accommodate them.

The Housing Authority Section 8 program is an excellent program for families who really need it. However, there are those who will always take advantage of the program which affords them the opportunity to get a decent place for themselves and their children. No Landlord rents a house or apartment thinking that the renter would eventually have to be evicted for not adhering to standard rules and regulations.

In those cases where some people would take advantage of the opportunity to have a decent place rent, they never seem to think about "what if I lose the opportunity to shelter me and my children". Their disregard places them back in the same position they were in prior to getting the help that they originally sought. There are always several people on a waiting list hoping to get a call that there is a home available for them and their families. As time goes on the negative behavior of some makes it difficult for others to get a place and they must remain on a waiting list, sometimes for years, before they can be called for a chance to get a place to live.